Celebrate life
and cook!

Nancy Mormar

To Many Cooks

MORE MEMORABLE MEALS

To Many Cooks

MORE MEMORABLE MEALS

NANCY WOOD MOORMAN

To Many Cooks
MORE MEMORABLE MEALS

Published by Nancy Wood Moorman

Copyright © 2007 by Nancy Wood Moorman
Too Many Cooks cooking school
340 Argyle Avenue
San Antonio, Texas 78209

Photography ©Tracy Maurer
Food Stylist: Rose Rankin
Back Cover Photo: Jeff Moorman

This cookbook is a collection of favorite recipes,
which are not necessarily original recipes.

ISBN 978-0-9788841-0-9
Library of Congress Control Number: 2006936410

Edited, Designed and Manufactured by
Favorite Recipes Press®
An imprint of

P.O. Box 305142
Nashville, Tennessee 37230
1-800-358-0560

Art Director and Book Design: Steve Newman
Editor: Jane Hinshaw
Project Editor: Nicki Pendleton Wood

First Printing: 2007
6000 copies
Printed in China

Contents

Dedication

To my husband, Jeff,
and my assistant, Sally,
whose recent battles with cancer
taught me about bravery.

Preface

I wrote my first cookbook, *Memorable Meals*, almost ten years ago. At that time, it never dawned on me that I would repeat that process—yet here I am. It is amazing to me what ten years does to each of us.

For me, the first eight years of this time were a period of real professional growth. Creating and interpreting recipes were exciting experiences. I experimented with new styles, techniques, and ingredients. I enjoyed my teaching. Cooking nurtured my soul while the food brought loved ones together in celebration. The last two years, however, were quite different. In 2004, within a three-month period, both my husband, Jeff, and my assistant, Sally, were diagnosed with cancer. I immediately stopped teaching to care for them. I stopped cooking almost completely. I cannot cook when trauma hits my life. It is not a conscious decision. It just happens. This phenomenon has always been a mystery to me.

Today, both Jeff and Sally are in remission. A year or so after this good news, I realized that I was reading recipes again. I began putting together this book. I began researching material for new classes. I became happy. I now realize why the kitchen becomes off limits when I am in crisis. Cooking for me is an act of pure joy. If the people I love are hurt, enjoying myself so thoroughly just doesn't make sense. Cooking has been a miracle for me. It is an act of creativity that fulfills the chef and an act of generosity that binds those participating. It stirs memories of my past and gives me the confidence to know that there are many more memories to be created.

It is nice now to be in a period of personal calm, when everyone I love is fine. I feel blessed to have had the joy to write this book. Hopefully it will encourage others to enjoy the cooking process. My desire is to take the mystique out of preparing food. If followed as written, each of these recipes can be prepared by a beginner.

Although the material for this book came together quite naturally, the title was another matter. After much debate and innumerable "pollings" of friends and family, *Too Many Cooks* became the title of choice. It seemed a natural, as that is the name of my cooking school. As you will notice, one subtle change was made as the title became "*To*" *Many Cooks*, which pleases me greatly. It represents my cooking school and my years of teaching while standing for much more. With this title I can truly say that this book is directed to the many cooks that have influenced my life, to the many cooks I have taught and to the future cooks I hope to influence. I toast all of them. I thank these cooks for kindling my passion for food and for keeping it as important to me today as when I first realized the magic of creating food to be shared. It is my hope that this book will help them create their own celebrations.

Fall Menus

A Welcome to Fall

Puff Pastry Bundles
Butternut Squash Soup
Cinnamon-Smoked Quail on Micro Greens with
Almonds, Merlot Cherries and Kalamata Vinaigrette
Upside-Down Pear Tart

Cooking Summer's Catch

Alaskan King Crab in Won Ton Cups
Red Snapper with Black-Eyed Pea and Citrus Salsa
Broiled Tomato
Fried Zucchini Strips with Tartar Sauce
Asian Coleslaw
Lemon Bars

Missed You over the Summer

Roquefort Pinwheels
Chicken Kiev
Penne with Mustard and Chives
Roasted Vegetables—Baby Zucchini and Squash
Mangoes, Ice Cream and Macaroons

Vegetarian Buffet

Wheat Berry Salad with Feta and Edamame
Herbed Cheese Torta
Swiss Chard, Spinach and Mushroom Cannelloni
Zucchini Rolls and Tomato Sauce
Fresh Mozzarella and Tomato Salad
Butterscotch Mousse Tart

Fall Menus

Halloween is for Adults, Too

Pizza Squares
Pork with New World Pan Sauce
Butternut Squash Tart
Creamy Polenta with Mascarpone
Frozen Pumpkin Mousse Torte

After the Hunt Brunch

Fresh Fruit
Turkey Hash with Waffles
Scrambled Eggs
Mixed Grill—Bacon and Sausage
Country-Style Biscuits
More Waffles with Maple Syrup

Thanksgiving with Friends

Smoked Salmon Panini
Poblano Soup with Corn and Avocado
Spiced Rubbed Venison
Baby Spinach Garlic Bread Pudding
Potato Gratin with Mushrooms and Leeks
French Tart with Apples and Nuts

Christmas Lunch

Cream of Mushroom Soup with Pastry Dome
Maple Peppered Turkey Breast
Festive Green Beans
French Mashed Potatoes
Corn Bread Terrine
Whipped Kahlúa Pie

Winter Menus

Family Reunion with Italian Flair

Parmesan Crisps with Smoked Duck
Roasted Garlic and Prosciutto Soup with Gruyère
Chicken Francese with Lemon and Pecorino
Saffron Orzo with Pesto
Carrot Flan
Gingersnap Cannoli

New Year's Eve

Smoked Salmon in Sesame Cones
Chicken and Pea Ravioli with Wild Mushroom Sauce
Lamb Rack with Provençal Crust
Creamed Fresh Spinach
French Mashed Potatoes
Salad Served in Parmesan Crisps
Chocolate and White Chocolate Mousse with
Crème Anglaise and Raspberry Sauce

Anniversary Celebration

Potato Latkes with Applesauce and Sour Cream
Asparagus Soup with Morel Custards
Beef Tenderloin with Stilton Sauce
Stir-Fry of Asparagus, Red Pepper and Snow Peas
White Beans with Fresh Herbs
Chocolate Truffle Cakes with Fresh Raspberries

Valentine Dinner

Cream Cheese Mold with Mango and Chutney
Creamy Duo of White Bean Soup and Carrot Soup with Heart Croutons
Chicken Saltimbocca and White Wine Sauce with Spinach Chiffonade
Spinach Soufflé Mold with Hollandaise (Heart-Shaped)
Double Cheese Potato Casserole
Chocolate and Raspberry Napoleons (Heart-Shaped)

Winter Menus

CHINESE NEW YEAR

Spring Rolls with Wild Mushrooms
Charred Shrimp with Red Ginger Barbecue Sauce on Arugula Salad
Spice Rubbed Seared Salmon
Fried Rice
Hunan Roasted Peppers
Ginger Cake with Brown Sugar Icing
Fortune Cookies

JANUARY BUFFET FOR SUPERBOWL

Pizza Squares
Chicken Curry with Steamed Rice and "The Boys"
Beef Stroganoff with Noodles
Large Salad
Mocha Orange Cheesecake

WINTER BUFFET CELEBRATING AN ENGAGEMENT

Ricotta Corn Cakes with Mushroom Salsa
Veal or Pork, Virginia Ham, Winter Vegetables and Fettucine
Individual Eggplant and Tomato Gratins
Large Salad with Hearts of Palm, Artichoke, Avocado-Caesar Dressing
Ricotta Cheese Bread
Crème Brûlée Napoleons

FAT TUESDAY—CELEBRATE MARDI GRAS

Shrimp Rangoon
Oysters and Scallops in Spinach Cream Sauce
Slow-Roasted Chicken au Poivre
Potato Pancakes with Gruyère
Green Beans with Pancetta and Pine Nuts
Crepes Suzette

Spring Menus

DERBY DAY

Mint Juleps
Smoky Bacon on Grits or Polenta
Plantation Okra
Carrot Fritters
Country Style Biscuits
Toasted Coconut Pie

OLD-FASHIONED AFTERNOON TEA
CELEBRATING A GRANDDAUGHTER

Cheesecake Dreams, Sugar Cookies, Bowl of Nuts and Colored Mints
Lemon Bars
Small Tea Sandwiches
Quiche Lorraine
Cold Poached Salmon Fillet with Sauce Verte
Chocolate Raspberry Napoleons

CLASSIC EASTER MENU

Cold Vichyssoise (Leek and Potato Soup)
Navarin of Lamb
Toasted Ricotta Bread
Frisée Salad with Vinaigrette
Carrot Cake

ST. PATRICK'S DAY, THE SOUTHWESTERN WAY

Green Pea Soup with Garnish of Peas, Avocado and Jicama
Grilled Chicken with Cilantro-Poblano and Ancho Sauces
Mexican Tomatillo Rice
Corn and Black Bean Ragout
Extra Green Piña Colada Mousse

Spring Menus

Final Four Basketball Playoffs

Fried Zucchini Strips
Cold Cauliflower Soup with Basil Oil
Manchurian Pork Chops
Double Cheese Potato Casserole
Stir-fry of Snow Peas, Asparagus and Red Pepper
Vincent Price's Diana Torte

Cinco de Mayo—A Mexican Fiesta

Goat Cheese Flautas
Grilled Shrimp and Black Bean Cake
Puffed Ancho Chiles with Guacamole
Wild Mushroom Enchiladas with Ancho Cream
Salad of Greens with Strawberries, Orange Slices and Jicama
Cajeta Flan Cake

Spring Dinner for Out-of-Town Guests

Meatballs with Sweet-and-Sour Sauce
Salmon Roulade with Tomato Beurre Blanc
Corn and Wild Mushroom Ragout
Eggplant and Tomato Gratin
Crème Brûlée Napoleons

Lunch Celebrating a Small Wedding

Parmesan Crisps with Smoked Duck
Gougonette of Sole with Tartar Sauce
Chicken Crepes
Spinach Soufflé Mold with Hollandaise
Salad with Fruit and French Vinaigrette
Almond Crunch Cake

Summer Menus

Kitchen Shower for Bride to Be

Cold Poached Salmon with Sauce Verte
Marinated Cucumbers
Cherry Tomato and Feta Salad with Walnuts and Basil
Sesame Chicken Salad with Radishes
Mango Tart

French Picnic on the Terrace

Salmon Tartare Layered in Individual Mold with
Mashed Avocado and Micro Greens
Red pepper Gazpacho with Lobster
Duck Confit Risotto
French Baguette
Black Plum Tart

Baby Shower Buffet

Senegalese Soup
Mushroom Quiche
Fresh Mozzarella Salad with Tomato and Basil
Watercress, Sweet Corn and Basmati Rice Salad with Grilled Shrimp
Lemon Curd Cake
Iced Motif Cookies

July Fourth

Katie's Ceviche with Chips
Pecan-Crusted Tilapia
Hominy Hash
Fresh Spinach
Coleslaw
Lemon-Lime Mousse with Mixed Berries
and Mangoes

Summer Menus

TOO HOT FOR DINNER—COME FOR COCKTAILS

Toast Points with Mascarpone and Fresh Mango
Fried Zucchini Strips with Herbed Mayonnaise
Smoked Salmon Tartare
Herbed Cheese Torta
Individual Grilled Baby Lamb Chops
Ricotta Corn Cakes with Mushroom Salsa
Medley of Pick Up Desserts

ITALIAN SUMMER DINNER

Ricotta Corn Cakes with Mushroom Salsa
Homemade Mozzarella and Tomato Stacks
Sea Bass with Asparagus Sauce
Hunan Roasted Peppers
Buttered Orzo with Saffron
Mangoes, Ice Cream and Macaroons

SUMMER LUNCH FOR BOOK CLUB

Golden Gazpacho with Rock Shrimp
Shrimp Congelia
Salad with Micro Greens, Jicama and Avocado
Ginger Ice Cream with Cookies

SO YOU'RE REALLY GOING TO ASIA

Tuna Sashimi in Sesame Cones
Mussels "The Thirsty Whale"
Thai Noodle Soup with Shrimp
Crisp Soft-Shell Crab with Asian Slaw
Ginger Cake

Appetizers and Small Plates

Charred Shrimp with Red Ginger Barbecue Sauce on Arugula Salad
Note Variation: Won Ton Napoleon (recipe on page 43)

TUNA SASHIMI IN SESAME CONES

MAKES 30

The sesame seed cones in this recipe are really a variation of a French lace cookie. They are delicate and should be made small enough to eat in one bite. You can substitute other sashimi, canned tuna, smoked salmon, or the filling you prefer for the uncooked tuna used here.

2 tablespoons white
   sesame seeds
2 tablespoons black
   sesame seeds
1 1/2 teaspoons ground ginger
1/2 teaspoon salt
1/4 cup (1/2 stick)
   unsalted butter
1/2 cup light corn syrup
1/2 cup all-purpose
   flour, sifted

SESAME CONES: Mix the white sesame seeds, black sesame seeds, ginger and salt in a medium bowl. Combine the butter with the corn syrup in a medium skillet and heat until the butter melts; do not allow the mixture to boil. Remove from the heat and add the flour and sesame seed mixture all at once, stirring to mix well.

Drop the mixture 1/2 teaspoon at a time on a nonstick baking mat, allowing six to a mat. Bake at 350 degrees until light brown, baking only one mat at a time. Cool slightly and form quickly into cones with your fingers. Cool to room temperature. Repeat with the remaining sesame batter.

2 tablespoons mayonnaise
1/2 teaspoon sriracha hot
   chili sauce
1 teaspoon sesame oil
1 teaspoon wasabi (optional)
8 ounces sushi-grade
   tuna, diced
1 teaspoon chopped
   pickled ginger
1 teaspoon chopped scallion

TUNA SASHIMI FILLING: Combine the mayonnaise, chili sauce, sesame oil and wasabi in a small bowl. Add the tuna, pickled ginger and scallion and mix gently. Chill until serving time.

TO SERVE: Spoon the tuna sashimi filling into the sesame cones and arrange on a serving dish. Garnish as desired.

NOTE: For sashimi, you should choose tuna that is very red in color; ask the butcher to cut the steak from a larger piece of fish. Freeze it for twenty-four hours or longer before using it. You can prepare the Sesame Cones in advance and freeze them in an airtight container. You can also leave the sesame disks flat and top with the filling.

FOREGROUND: *Tuna Sashimi in Sesame Cones*
   Note Variation: fresh salmon
BACKGROUND: *Parmesan Crisps with Smoked Duck*

CREAM CHEESE MOLD WITH MANGO CHUTNEY

SERVES 24

*A few days before mailing this book to the printer, I served this
dish for company at our ranch in Brady, Texas. It met with such rave
reviews that I decided to add it to the list of appetizers. I give
credit for the original idea to a friend from Dallas.*

8 (8-ounce) packages cream
   cheese, softened
Juice of 1 lemon
1 cup chopped scallions

CREAM CHEESE MOLD: Combine half the cream cheese
with half the lemon juice in a food processor fitted
with a steel blade. Process until smooth. Spread the
mixture in a 9-inch springform pan and sprinkle with
the scallions. Process the remaining cream cheese and
lemon juice until smooth and spread over the scallions.
Cover with plastic wrap and chill for 2 to 12 hours or
until firm.

1 to 2 cups mango chutney
1 to 2 cups cashews,
   coarsely chopped

TO ASSEMBLE AND SERVE: Place the springform pan
on a platter and remove the side. Spread the chutney
over the top and sprinkle with the cashews. Serve
cold with crackers.

*VARIATION: Use your imagination to vary this dish. Use a
different chutney, add mascarpone cheese to the cream
cheese, or add blue cheese and top with pear chutney.*

Toast Points with Mascarpone and Fresh Mango

Serves 24

*It is a treasure to find new appetizers that can be assembled before
guests arrive and served cold. This basic recipe can be
varied in many ways, such as substituting melon balls for the
mango or tiny shrimp for the fruit and ham.*

**6 slices Pepperidge Farm very
thin whole wheat bread**
**1/4 to 1/2 cup (1/2 to 1 stick)
butter**

TOAST POINTS: Cut each bread slice into four triangles
or into rounds with a 1- to 2-inch cutter. Add enough
butter to a sauté pan to lightly coat as many pieces of
bread as will easily fit in the pan at once. Cook over
medium heat until brown on both sides. Remove to a
paper towel and repeat with the remaining butter and
bread. Use immediately or store in an airtight container
and reheat at 350 degrees to crisp before serving.

**6 ounces mascarpone cheese
or cream cheese**
1 tablespoon Dijon mustard
Salt to taste

MASCARPONE TOPPING: Combine the mascarpone cheese
and Dijon mustard in a bowl and mix well. Season to
taste with salt.

Prosciutto or salami slices
1 mango, peeled
Fresh mint

TO ASSEMBLE AND SERVE: Cut the prosciutto to fit the
toast points. Cut the mango into 1/4-inch cubes. Slice the
mint into a thin chiffonade. Spread the mascarpone
topping over the toast points, reserving a small amount.
Add the prosciutto and top with the reserved topping
to hold the mango. Sprinkle with the mango and top
with the mint.

HERBED CHEESE TORTA WITH OLIVE BREAD

SERVES 8

In the spring of 2003, I led a group to the Greenbrier in West Virginia to attend a three-day cooking school. This has been the recipe most used by all who attended. Make your life easy by serving it with an olive bread purchased at the bakery in many good markets.

1/2 cup fresh basil leaves
2 tablespoons grated
   Parmesan cheese
1 tablespoon toasted pine nuts
1 garlic clove, minced
1/4 teaspoon kosher salt
1 tablespoon olive oil
3 tablespoons mascarpone
   cheese or cream cheese

BASIL PESTO LAYER: Combine the basil, Parmesan cheese, pine nuts, garlic and kosher salt in a food processor and process until the basil is very finely chopped. Add the olive oil through the feed tube gradually, processing constantly until smooth. Add the mascarpone cheese and process to mix well. Taste and correct the seasoning if needed. Chill until time to assemble.

5.2 ounces boursin
   cheese, softened
1/4 cup heavy cream

BOURSIN LAYER: Combine the boursin cheese with the cream in a mini-food processor and process until smooth. Chill until time to assemble.

1 garlic clove
1/3 cup parsley
1 to 2 tablespoons grated
   Parmesan cheese
1/4 cup packed
   sun-dried tomatoes
2 tablespoons herbed
   tomato paste
Salt and pepper to taste

SUN-DRIED TOMATO LAYER: Combine the garlic and parsley in a mini-food processor. Process until minced. Add the Parmesan cheese, sun-dried tomatoes and tomato paste; process until smooth. Season with salt and pepper.

Fresh basil sprigs
Toasted olive bread

TO ASSEMBLE AND SERVE: Line a 4-inch springform pan with plastic wrap (and spray the plastic wrap with nonstick cooking spray). Layer the basil pesto mixture, the boursin mixture and the sun-dried tomato mixture in the prepared pan, smoothing each layer and pressing down gently to pack evenly. Chill for 30 minutes or up to 24 hours. Invert the torta onto a serving platter and remove the plastic wrap. Smooth the top with a knife dipped in water. Garnish with fresh basil and serve with toasted olive bread.

Parmesan Crisps with Smoked Duck

Makes 10 to 12

*I discovered these crisps years ago at Daniel Bouloud's Restaurant
Daniel in New York. They are now very easy to make thanks to the use
of a nonstick baking mat, such as Silpat®. I have brought the entire dish
down to earth by using Heinz 57 sauce as the secret ingredient.*

**¹/₂ cup finely grated fresh
Parmiagiano-Reggiano cheese**

PARMESAN CRISPS: Line a baking sheet with a nonstick baking mat. Sprinkle 2 teaspoons of the Parmesan cheese in one corner of the baking sheet and spread into a 2-inch circle with a small spoon. Repeat to make about twelve circles. Bake at 325 degrees for 8 to 10 minutes or until golden brown. Transfer to paper towels with a small spatula and mold into cups over the bottoms of miniature muffin cups while still warm. Let stand until cool and crisp. Store in an airtight container for up to 2 days or freeze until needed.

**1 purchased smoked
duck breast
¹/₂ cup mayonnaise
1 to 2 tablespoons
Heinz 57 sauce**

DUCK FILLING: Place the duck in a baking pan and heat in a 350-degree oven for about 30 minutes. Cool slightly and cut into small pieces, discarding the skin.

Combine with the mayonnaise and Heinz 57 in a small bowl and mix well.

**Tiny sprigs of parsley or
Italian parsley, microgreens
or chopped chives**

TO ASSEMBLE AND SERVE: Spoon the duck filling into the Parmesan crisp cups and garnish with a sprig of parsley.

VARIATION: You can also leave the Parmesan Crisps flat and top with the duck filling or make them larger to serve with a salad.

Spring Rolls with Wild Mushrooms

Serves 8 to 10

The incredible flavor in this dish is a fusion of French
wild mushrooms with Asian spices. I would like to give Karen Lee,
a wonderful Asian Fusion teacher in New York, credit for
introducing me to this special dish!

---

1 teaspoon cornstarch
1 tablespoon dry sherry
2 tablespoons dark soy sauce
2 tablespoons oyster sauce

SEASONING SAUCE: Dissolve the cornstarch in the sherry in a small bowl. Add the soy sauce and oyster sauce; mix well.

---

¹/₂ cup dried mixed
   wild mushrooms
1 cup hot water
1 or 2 large leeks
3 tablespoons peanut oil
8 ounces mixed fresh
   wild mushrooms

MUSHROOM FILLING: Combine the dried mushrooms with the water in a bowl and let stand for 30 minutes. Drain and press to remove the moisture. Chop the mushrooms.

Split the leeks lengthwise and wash well. Chop and measure 3 cups. Heat a wok over high heat for about 1 minute or until smoking. Add the peanut oil and heat until hot but not smoking. Add the leeks and stir-fry for 2 minutes or until limp. Add the fresh mushrooms and stir-fry for 1 minute. Add the chopped reconstituted mushrooms and seasoning sauce. Cook until all the liquid has evaporated. Place in a colander to cool and drain well to avoid breaking the spring roll wrappers.

---

8 to 10 frozen spring
   roll wrappers
3 cups vegetable oil

SPRING ROLLS: Wrap the frozen spring roll wrappers in a damp kitchen towel to thaw at cooking time. Separate and stack in a damp towel to prevent drying.

Place one wrapper at a time on a work surface and place 2 to 3 tablespoons of the mushroom filling in the center. Brush the sides and top with water. Fold in the sides and roll the wrapper from the bottom; press to seal.

Heat the vegetable oil in a hot wok. Add the spring rolls five at a time. Cook for about 3 minutes or until golden brown, turning once. Drain on paper towels, cut into halves diagonally and arrange on a serving platter.

NOTE: You can prepare the spring rolls in advance and fry for one minute. Fry for two minutes longer at serving time. To hold for up to 24 hours, fry for one minute and store, uncovered, in the refrigerator until time to reheat. They can also be frozen and fried directly from the freezer.

Pizza Squares with Fresh Mozzarella

Makes 20 to 30

*Pizza made from frozen puff pastry is amazingly easy and
delicious. Add homemade tomato sauce and sliced fresh mozzarella.
Embellish the squares with different herbs, shrimp, olives,
or any ingredient that suits your fancy.*

1/2 cup minced onion
2 garlic cloves, minced
2 to 3 tablespoons olive oil
1 (28-ounce) can
   tomatoes, chopped
2 tablespoons tomato paste
1 bay leaf
1 teaspoon dried
   oregano, crushed
2 sprigs parsley
1/2 cup water

HOMEMADE TOMATO SAUCE: Sauté the onion and garlic in the olive oil in a 3-quart saucepan for 3 minutes or until translucent. Add the tomatoes, tomato paste, bay leaf, oregano, parsley and water; mix well. Cook over medium heat for 30 minutes or until thickened. Remove from the heat and discard the bay leaf. Purée in a blender or food processor. Return to the saucepan and simmer for 30 minutes longer if necessary for the desired consistency.

---

1 sheet frozen puff
   pastry, thawed

PIZZA CRUST: Roll the puff pastry into a rectangle as thin as possible on a work surface. (If using Dufour puff pastry, it is not necessary to roll it.) Spray nonstick cooking spray on a 9×12-inch baking sheet with low sides. Fit the pastry into the baking sheet and prick in many places with a fork to prevent puffing. Bake at 400 degrees for 15 minutes or until brown. Prick the pastry again and turn it over. Bake the other side until brown; cool.

---

4 to 6 slices bacon, crisp-fried
   and crumbled
1/2 cup chopped
   sun-dried tomatoes
Grated Parmesan cheese
Sliced fresh mozzarella cheese
Olive oil

TO FINISH AND SERVE: Spread 3/4 cup of the homemade tomato sauce on the pizza crust. Sprinkle with the bacon, sun-dried tomatoes and Parmesan cheese. Cover with 1 1/2 cups of the homemade tomato sauce. Arrange the sliced mozzarella cheese over the top and sprinkle with additional Parmesan cheese. Drizzle with olive oil. Bake at 400 degrees for 20 to 30 minutes or until bubbly. Cut into squares to serve.

SMOKED SALMON PANINI

MAKES 6

*Panini have become quite popular and have endless variations.
Do not be put off by the fancy name; it is just a dressed-up grilled
sandwich. You can use a simple grill pan and spatula if
you do not have a panini press.*

8 ounces thinly sliced
  smoked salmon
12 slices firm white sandwich
  bread, crusts trimmed, or
  12 slices Pepperidge Farm
  rye bread
1 tablespoon finely
  chopped chives
6 ounces Gruyère cheese,
  very thinly sliced
1/2 cup (1 stick) unsalted
  butter, softened

Arrange the salmon on six of the bread slices and
sprinkle with the chives. Top with the cheese and the
remaining bread slices. Spread the tops of the
sandwiches with half the butter. Heat a 12-inch skillet
until hot and add three sandwiches at a time, placing
the buttered side down. Cook for 3 to 4 minutes or
until the bottoms are golden brown and the cheese
begins to melt. Spread the tops with the remaining
butter and turn the sandwiches over. Cook for
1 minute longer or until light brown. Cut the sandwiches
into quarters diagonally and serve immediately.

*NOTE: You can also prepare these in advance. Place on a
baking sheet and reheat at 350 degrees for 10 minutes.*

SMOKED SALMON TARTARE

SERVES 15 TO 20

Salmon Tartare is a beautiful appetizer for a cocktail party.
Mold it in a ring or a shape keyed to the holiday, such as a heart mold
for Valentine's Day or a star for Christmas.

1 (1½-pound) smoked
   salmon fillet
1 cucumber, peeled and seeded
1 red bell pepper, seeded
1 yellow bell pepper, seeded
1 shallot
1 to 3 tablespoons chopped
   dill weed
1 tablespoon Dijon mustard
¼ cup white wine vinegar
½ to ¾ cup mayonnaise
Juice of 1 lemon
Salt and pepper to taste

SALMON TARTARE: Chop the salmon, cucumber, red bell pepper, yellow bell pepper and shallot finely. Combine with the dill weed in a large bowl. Add the Dijon mustard, vinegar, mayonnaise and lemon juice and mix well. Season with salt and pepper.

Place a ring mold on a flat baking sheet and pack the salmon mixture evenly into the ring. Chill for 3 to 12 hours.

TO SERVE: Remove the ring from the salmon mixture and slide the molded salmon tartare onto a serving plate. Decorate as desired. Serve with individual toast points or crackers. To pass individually, you can also spoon it onto crisp potato chips or into tiny tart shells.

VARIATION: Serve as a first course by molding in 2-inch rings and topping with seasoned chopped avocado and a sprig of microgreens. Place on serving plates, remove the rings and serve with a good vinaigrette and dots of basil oil. You can also substitute lightly poached salmon for half of the smoked salmon.

Goat Cheese Flautas with Diablo Sauce

Makes 24

*Use won ton wrappers instead of the traditional
tortillas to produce a perfect single serving hors d'oeuvre.
Your guests will be pleasantly surprised.*

1 tablespoon vegetable oil
3 shallots, chopped
3 garlic cloves, chopped
1 serrano chile
1 teaspoon cumin seeds
1 tablespoon grated ginger
2 red bell peppers, seeded
   and chopped
1/2 mango, chopped
1 cup chicken stock
Lime juice to taste
Salt to taste

DIABLO SAUCE: Heat the vegetable oil in a skillet until lightly smoking. Add the shallots, garlic and chile and sauté until light brown. Add the cumin seeds, ginger and red bell peppers. Sauté for 30 seconds. Stir in the mango and chicken stock. Reduce the heat and simmer for 20 minutes. Purée the mixture in a food processor or with a hand blender. Season with lime juice and salt. Store in the refrigerator until needed and serve hot or cold.

8 ounces goat cheese, or a
   mixture of equal parts goat
   cheese and cream cheese
1 egg
1/2 cup chopped cilantro
1 teaspoon salt
1/2 teaspoon pepper
24 won ton wrappers
2 cups vegetable oil

FLAUTAS: Combine the goat cheese, egg, cilantro, salt and pepper in a food processor and process until smooth. Spoon 1 teaspoon of the cheese mixture onto one end of each won ton wrapper. Fold the sides in and brush the edges with water. Roll to enclose the filling and press to seal. Heat the vegetable oil in a large saucepan and add the flautas in batches. Fry until golden brown and then drain. Serve hot with the diablo sauce.

ALASKAN KING CRAB IN WON TON CUPS

MAKES 24

You will find these cups are great containers for a variety of appetizers. The filling is indicative of the popularity of appetizers inspired by Asian flavors.

---

24 won ton wrappers
Salt to taste

WON TON CUPS: Stack half the won ton wrappers together at a time and trim the stacks into 3-inch squares. Form cups by pressing the wrappers gently into miniature muffin cups sprayed with nonstick cooking spray. Spray the wrappers with nonstick cooking spray and sprinkle with salt. Bake at 375 degrees for 7 to 10 minutes or until golden brown and crisp. Remove to a wire rack to cool and continue to crisp. Store in an airtight container for up to 2 days.

---

1 ripe avocado
1¹/₂ teaspoons finely
chopped shallot
1 tablespoon lime juice
¹/₄ to ¹/₂ teaspoon wasabi
Chopped cilantro (optional)
Salt and pepper to taste

AVOCADO FILLING: Scoop the avocado from the skin into a bowl and mash. Add the shallot, lime juice, wasabi and cilantro. Season with salt and pepper and mix gently. Store in the refrigerator for up to 4 hours.

---

4 ounces Alaskan King
crab meat in the shell,
cooked
1 tablespoon lime juice
Salt to taste

TO ASSEMBLE AND SERVE: Remove the crab meat from the shell and cut into ¹/₂-inch pieces. Toss with the lime juice in a bowl and season with salt. Spoon the avocado mixture into the won ton cups. Top with the crab meat and serve immediately.

SHRIMP WON TONS WITH MANGO SALSA

SERVES 6 TO 8

Once again, Asian ingredients are flavoring this first course.
The colors are amazing: orange mangos, green basil, dark hoisin sauce.
I usually serve this as a first course because the mango salsa is
a little hard to manage standing up. If you do want to serve the shrimp
as an appetizer, pass them on a tray with a good chutney, Asian
dipping sauce, or wasabi for dipping.

1 large ripe mango, chopped
1/3 to 1/2 cup minced onion
1/2 cup loosely packed
   chopped cilantro
1/4 cup red wine vinegar
1 tablespoon soy sauce

MANGO SALSA: Combine the mango, onion and cilantro in a medium bowl and mix well. Stir in the vinegar and soy sauce. Store in the refrigerator.

1 cup soy sauce
1/2 cup sesame oil
1 (3-inch) piece
   ginger, peeled
1/2 cup loosely packed cilantro
24 large shrimp, peeled
   and deveined

MARINATED SHRIMP: Combine the soy sauce, sesame oil, ginger and cilantro in a blender and process until smooth. Combine with the shrimp in a dish and marinate for 15 minutes or longer; drain.

24 won ton wrappers
24 fresh basil leaves
8 to 12 cups vegetable oil

WON TONS: Place the won ton wrappers one at a time on a work surface. Top each with a basil leaf and a marinated shrimp. Roll the won ton to enclose the basil and shrimp, tucking in the edges to secure the filling. Heat the vegetable oil in a deep fryer until hot but not smoking. Deep-fry the won tons in batches for 2 minutes or until golden brown. You may also arrange the won tons on a plate and cover with plastic wrap to prevent sticking; store in the refrigerator to fry later.

Hoisin sauce
Chopped cilantro

TO SERVE: Place three or four won tons on each large dinner plate and spoon the mango salsa on one side. Pipe hoisin sauce in a decorative pattern over the won tons and sprinkle with cilantro.

SHRIMP OR CRAB RANGOON

MAKES 24

*These fried bite-size won tons are a great taste treat.
I found a wonderful wasabi-ginger sauce made by Stonewall
Kitchens to use as a dipping sauce with them.*

4 ounces shrimp or crab meat
4 ounces cream cheese
1 garlic clove, minced
3/4 teaspoon A.1. steak sauce
1/3 cup chopped cilantro
Salt and pepper to taste

SHRIMP FILLING: Combine the shrimp, cream cheese, garlic, steak sauce and cilantro in a food processor; process until smooth and season with salt and pepper.

24 square won ton wrappers
6 cups vegetable oil
Wasabi-ginger sauce or other
    dipping sauce

RANGOON: Place one won ton wrapper at a time on a work surface with one corner pointing toward you. Spoon 1 teaspoon of the shrimp filling into the center of each wrapper and moisten the edges with water. Fold the wrappers to form triangles and press the edges to seal. Press the sides up toward the centers to form packets. Heat the vegetable oil in a medium saucepan or wok until hot but not smoking. Add the won tons in batches and deep-fry until golden brown. Drain on paper towels and serve with dipping sauce.

SHRIMP CONGELIA

SERVES 6 TO 8

*Shrimp Congelia is a rich dish that is easy to prepare. You can also
serve it with your favorite salad for an elegant light lunch.*

1 pound shrimp, cooked
2/3 cup mayonnaise
1/3 cup ketchup
2 tablespoons horseradish
1/4 cup chopped chives
Juice of 1 lemon
Scallop shells
Toasted bread crumbs
Grated Parmesan cheese
Butter

Peel the shrimp and cut into 1/2-inch pieces. Mix with the mayonnaise, ketchup, horseradish, chives and lemon juice in a bowl. Spoon into buttered scallop shells and sprinkle with a mixture of bread crumbs and Parmesan cheese; dot with butter. Bake at 400 degrees until heated through and the tops are brown. Broil for 1 or 2 minutes to brown the tops if needed. Serve in the shells.

BLT Cherry Tomatoes

Serves 5

I credit these to Sally Helland, my assistant, who serves them often when she caters. The only time-consuming part is scooping out the tomatoes, but you will find it worth the effort.

10 cherry tomatoes
Salt to taste

TOMATO SHELLS: Cut a 1/4-inch slice off the top of each cherry tomato with a serrated knife. Scoop out the pulp and seeds carefully. Sprinkle the shells lightly with salt and invert onto paper towels for 15 minutes to drain.

4 slices bacon, crisp-fried
    and crumbled
1/4 cup finely shredded lettuce
2 tablespoons thinly
    sliced scallions
2 tablespoons mayonnaise
Salt and pepper to taste

BACON FILLING: Combine the bacon, lettuce, scallions and mayonnaise in a small bowl and mix well. Season with salt and pepper.

TO ASSEMBLE AND SERVE: Spoon the bacon filling into the tomato shells and arrange on a platter. Store, covered, in the refrigerator until time to serve. Serve cold.

PUFF PASTRY BUNDLES WITH BLUE CHEESE AND PEAR

MAKES 25 TO 30

*New appetizers are always an exciting find. This recipe was given
to me by a golfing friend in Palm Springs. The combination
of blue cheese and pear is a natural. Their appeal is further enhanced
by the fact that they are best prepared in advance, frozen and
taken directly from the freezer to the oven at serving time.*

1 sheet frozen puff pastry,
   thawed
1 egg
1 tablespoon water
4 ounces blue cheese

BUNDLES: Roll the puff pastry very thin on a work
surface. Cut into 2×3-inch rectangles. Beat the egg
with the water in a cup and brush onto the pastry
rectangles.

   Shape the blue cheese into balls and place one
ball in the center of each pastry rectangle. Bring up
the opposite corners to enclose the cheese and press
to seal. Arrange on a baking tray and freeze, covered,
until time to bake. Bake the frozen bundles at
400 degrees for 8 to 12 minutes or until brown
and puffed.

1 pear
1 to 2 cups water
Juice of 1 lemon

TO ASSEMBLE AND SERVE: Cut the pear into small cubes
and add to a mixture of the water and lemon juice in
a bowl until time to serve; drain. Arrange the baked
bundles on a serving plate and place one pear cube at
the center of each bundle.

*VARIATION: Change this dish by crumbling blue cheese over
a sheet of puff pastry, leaving a one-inch border on all
sides. Brush the edges with beaten egg and roll the pastry to
enclose the cheese. Cut into 12 to 16 slices and bake at
400 degrees for 15 minutes or until brown.*

CHICKEN AND SWEET PEA RAVIOLI WITH WILD MUSHROOM SAUCE

SERVES 8 TO 10

*When I began teaching, this dish was done using fresh pasta,
which is still an option, but the availability of won ton wrappers makes
the dish easy for everyone to do. I have included two sauces, but
have only used the Sweet Pea Sauce as a garnish, so if time is short,
you can serve the ravioli with the Wild Mushroom Sauce alone.*

8 ounces dried mixed whole
   wild mushrooms
1 to 2 ounces dried morels
2 tablespoons olive oil
1/2 onion, finely chopped
2 garlic cloves, minced
16 ounces shiitake
   mushrooms, sliced
1/4 cup (1/2 stick) butter
1/4 cup all-purpose flour
3 to 4 cups beef broth
1 tablespoon beef extract
Salt and pepper to taste

WILD MUSHROOM SAUCE: Combine the dried mushrooms with hot water in a bowl and let stand to reconstitute. Heat the olive oil in a large sauté pan. Add the onion and garlic and sauté over medium heat until tender. Add the shiitake mushrooms and sauté briefly. Squeeze the water from the wild mushroom and add the mushroms to the sauté pan; sauté until tender. Add the butter and cook until the butter melts. Stir in the flour and cook for 1 to 2 minutes. Add the beef broth and increase the heat. Cook until thickened, stirring constantly. Stir in the beef extract and season with salt and pepper.

1/3 cup chopped shallots
1 garlic clove, chopped
2 tablespoons unsalted butter
1/2 russet potato, peeled
   and chopped
1 to 2 cups vegetable broth or
   chicken broth
2 cups frozen peas, thawed
Salt and pepper to taste

SWEET PEA SAUCE: Sauté the shallots and garlic in the heated butter in a large saucepan over medium heat. Add the potato and broth. Cook until the potato is tender. Purée the peas in a blender. Add the potato mixture and process until very smooth. Season with salt and pepper. Press through a strainer into the saucepan.

1 cup frozen baby peas, thawed
3 garlic cloves
2 boneless skinless
   chicken breasts
2 eggs
1 teaspoon water
1 package won ton wrappers,
   or egg roll wrappers for
   larger ravioli
4 to 5 ounces goat cheese

RAVIOLI: Process the peas and garlic in a food processor until minced. Add the chicken and process to mix well. Add one of the eggs and process to a smooth paste.

Beat the remaining egg with the water in a cup. Place 1 won ton wrapper at a time on a work surface and brush with the egg mixture. Spoon 1 teaspoon of the chicken mixture into each of the four quadrants of the wrappers. Top each with 1/4 teaspoon of the goat cheese, pressing to flatten the mixture. Add a second won ton wrapper, stretching it to fit over the filling and seal the edges. Trim the edges and cut each square into four ravioli with a knife or fluted cutter. Place on a tray lined with baking parchment. Cook the ravioli in boiling water in a saucepan until cooked through; drain.

Chopped chives
Finely chopped and sautéed
   red bell pepper
Chopped fresh basil
1/2 cup peas

TO ASSEMBLE AND SERVE: Reheat the wild mushroom sauce and sweet pea sauce. Place the ravioli on a serving plate and top with the wild mushroom sauce. Dot the plate with the sweet pea sauce. Garnish with chopped chives, red bell pepper, basil and/or the peas.

CHICKEN CREPES

MAKES 15 TO 20

When I began teaching in 1977, you had to know French techniques to be considered a sophisticated cook, and crepe-making was a must. This recipe is for traditional chicken crepes, but do not UNDERESTIMATE ITS VALUE: it can be a springboard for your own new creations.

2 whole chicken breasts
1 piece of onion
1 piece of celery
1 bay leaf
1 teaspoon ground oregano
Salt and pepper to taste
6 tablespoons butter
8 to 12 ounces
   mushrooms, sliced
6 tablespoons all-purpose flour
3 to 4 cups milk

CREPE FILLING: Combine the chicken with the onion, celery, bay leaf, oregano, salt, pepper and enough water to cover in a saucepan. Cook for 20 to 25 minutes or until tender. Drain, discarding the vegetables and bay leaf. Cut the chicken into 1/2-inch pieces, discarding the skin and bones.

Melt the butter in a 3-quart saucepan and add the mushrooms. Sauté until tender. Add the flour and cook for 1 to 2 minutes, stirring constantly. Add 3 cups of milk all at once and increase the heat to medium-high. Cook until thickened, whisking constantly and adding additional milk if necessary for the desired consistency. Season with salt and pepper. Add the chicken and mix well.

2 eggs
1 cup all-purpose flour
2 tablespoons butter, melted
   and cooled
1 teaspoon salt
1 1/4 to 1 1/2 cups milk
melted butter

CREPES: Combine the eggs and flour in a food processor and process until smooth. Add 2 tablespoons butter and the salt and mix well. Add the milk through the feed tube and process until smooth, scraping down the side of the bowl as necessary. Pour into a measuring cup.

Brush a crepe pan with melted butter and place over medium-high heat. Add just enough crepe batter to cover the bottom of the pan, swirling to cover evenly. Cook until the top appears nearly dry and turn the crepe over. Cook for several seconds or just until cooked through. Repeat until all the batter is used, stacking the crepes as they cook.

1 to 2 cups (4 to 8 ounces)
   shredded Swiss cheese
2 to 3 cups heavy cream

TO FINISH AND SERVE: Spoon the filling onto the crepes and roll to enclose the filling. Arrange seam side down in a baking dish and sprinkle with the Swiss cheese. Add enough cream to almost cover the crepes. Bake at 400 degrees for 30 to 40 minutes or until the cream is thickened. Serve immediately.

Fried Zucchini Strips with Herbed Mayonnaise

Serves 4 to 6

There are many variations of this recipe, but after experimenting, I discovered that this batter of equal parts flour and beer produced the lightest and crispiest fritters.

1 cup mayonnaise or
    sour cream
Juice of 1/2 lemon
1/2 cup minced fresh basil
Seasoned salt to taste
2 or 3 drops of Tabasco sauce

HERBED MAYONNAISE: Combine the mayonnaise, lemon juice, basil and seasoned salt in a bowl and mix well. Add the Tabasco sauce and mix well. Store in the refrigerator.

1 cup all-purpose flour
1 cup beer
1 teaspoon salt
2 to 3 tablespoons chopped
    fresh basil (optional)
2 medium zucchini
3 to 4 cups vegetable oil
Salt to taste

ZUCCHINI STRIPS: Combine the flour, beer and 1 teaspoon salt in a bowl and whisk until smooth. Stir in the basil and let the batter rest for 1 hour. Stir the batter and thin with additional beer if it appears too thick. Cut the zucchini into eight spears. Heat the vegetable oil in a saucepan until hot but not smoking. Dip the zucchini into the batter and fry in the heated oil for 2 minutes or until deep golden brown. Drain on paper towels and season with salt while hot. Serve immediately with the herbed mayonnaise.

Swiss Chard, Spinach and Mushroom Cannelloni

Serves 6 to 8

*Many recipes today are simply a whimsical play on words. Here we
have cannelloni made with crepes instead of noodles.*

2 to 4 ounces dried wild
   mushrooms
2 to 3 tablespoons olive oil
2 garlic cloves, minced
3/4 cup chopped green onions
1 red bell pepper, chopped
16 ounces fresh wild
   mushrooms, coarsely
   chopped
6 tablespoons butter
6 tablespoons all-purpose flour
4 to 5 cups beef broth or
   chicken broth
Salt and pepper to taste
1 to 2 cups beef broth or
   chicken broth

MUSHROOM SAUCE: Combine the dried mushrooms
with hot water in a bowl and let stand for 15 minutes
to reconstitute. Heat the olive oil in a 3-quart saucepan
over medium heat. Add the garlic, green onions and
red bell pepper and sauté until tender. Add the fresh
mushrooms and sauté until cooked through. Drain and
chop the reconstituted mushrooms, reserving the soaking
liquid. Add the chopped reconstituted mushrooms to
the saucepan.

Add the butter and cook until it melts. Stir in the
flour well. Add 4 to 5 cups broth and cook over
medium-high heat until thickened, stirring constantly.
Add the reserved mushroom soaking liquid if needed
for the desired consistency. Season with salt and pepper.

Remove half the mixture to another saucepan and
stir in an additional 1 to 2 cups broth. Cook over
medium heat until of sauce consistency. Set aside and
keep warm.

1/2 to 3/4 cup (2 to 3 ounces)
   mixed shredded mozzarella
   cheese and
   grated Parmesan cheese
1 tablespoon salt
1 bunch Swiss chard,
   stems removed
1 tablespoon salt
2 bunches spinach,
   stems removed

CANNELLONI FILLING: Combine the remaining hot
mushroom sauce with the cheese in a bowl; mix to melt
the cheese. Bring 2 inches water to a boil in a large
saucepan and add 1 tablespoon salt. Add the Swiss
chard and cook, covered, for 10 to 12 minutes or until
tender. Drain, cool and chop the chard. Add to the
mushroom sauce in the bowl.

Bring 2 inches water to a boil in a large saucepan
and add 1 tablespoon salt. Add the spinach and cook
for 1 to 2 minutes or until tender. Drain, cool and
chop the spinach. Add to the mushroom sauce in
the bowl.

1 tablespoon melted butter
1 cup all-purpose flour
2 eggs
1/2 teaspoon salt
1/4 cup milk
Melted butter

CREPES: Combine 1 tablespoon butter, the flour, eggs and salt in a food processor and process for 5 seconds or until mixed. Add the milk through the feed tube, processing constantly for 1 minute or until smooth, scraping the bowl as needed. Spoon into a measuring cup. Brush a crepe pan with butter and add just enough batter to cover the bottom, swirling the pan to cover evenly. Cook for 1 minute or until dry and turn the crepe. Cook just until cooked through. Remove and stack on a plate. Repeat with the remaining batter.

Grated Parmesan cheese
Shredded mozzarella cheese

TO FINISH AND SERVE: Spoon 2 tablespoons of the cannelloni filling onto each crepe and sprinkle with additional Parmesan cheese. Roll the crepes to enclose the filling and place seam side down in a baking dish. Spoon the reserved mushroom sauce over the crepes and top with additional mozzarella cheese. Store in the refrigerator until time to bake. Bake at 350 degrees or until bubbly and light brown. Serve immediately as a first course or side dish.

VARIATION: The Swiss chard adds texture to this dish, but you can substitute additional spinach for the chard if you prefer.

WILD MUSHROOM ENCHILADAS WITH ANCHO CREAM

SERVES 8

The combination of corn tortillas, wild mushrooms, feta cheese,
avocados, and ancho cream sauce turns out to be a great taste treat that
can be used as a first course or as a vegetarian one-dish meal.

2 dried ancho chiles
2 cups boiling water
4 garlic cloves
2 cups heavy cream
4 teaspoons fresh lime juice
Salt to taste

ANCHO CREAM SAUCE: Soak the ancho chiles in the water for 30 minutes. Drain the chiles, reserving $1/3$ cup of the soaking liquid. Slice the chiles open and discard the stems and seeds. Combine the chiles with the reserved liquid and garlic in a blender and process until smooth. Combine with the cream in a large heavy skillet and bring to a boil. Reduce the heat and simmer for 3 minutes. Whisk in the lime juice and season with salt. Strain and return to the saucepan.

2 to 4 ounces dried wild
   mushrooms
3 tablespoons butter
$3/4$ cup chopped onion
$1^1/2$ pounds fresh wild
   mushrooms, sliced
5 ounces feta cheese, crumbled
2 tomatoes, seeded
   and chopped
6 tablespoons chopped
   fresh cilantro
1 small avocado, cut into
   $1/2$-inch pieces
Salt and pepper to taste
8 (6-inch) corn tortillas

ENCHILADAS: Combine the dried mushrooms with hot water in a bowl and let stand to reconstitute. Melt the butter in a large heavy skillet over medium heat. Add the onion and fresh mushrooms and sauté for 5 minutes or until the onion is translucent and the mushrooms are tender. Drain and chop the dried mushrooms. Add to the skillet with the feta cheese, tomatoes, cilantro and 6 tablespoons of the ancho cream sauce. Simmer for 4 minutes or just until heated through. Stir in the avocado and season with salt and pepper. Remove from the heat.

Bring the remaining ancho cream sauce to a simmer over low heat. Dip the tortillas one at a time into the sauce for 15 seconds or until softened, turning to coat evenly; cover the sauce and keep warm when not in use. Place the tortillas on a plate and spoon $1/3$ cup of the mushroom mixture down the center of each tortilla. Roll the tortillas to enclose the filling and arrange seam side down in a baking dish. Cover with the remaining sauce. Bake, covered with foil, at 350 degrees for 10 to 20 minutes or until heated through. Serve immediately.

MEATBALLS WITH SWEET-AND-SOUR SAUCE

MAKES 48 MEATBALLS

*Meatballs sound like mundane fare, but you cannot make
enough of these for a crowd; it's inevitable you will run out. I credit this
recipe to Patsy, my neighbor of many years.*

4 ounces ground beef
4 ounces ground pork
1/4 cup finely chopped
   water chestnuts
2 garlic cloves, minced
1/2 cup rolled oats
1/2 cup milk
1 tablespoon Worcestershire
   sauce
1/2 teaspoon garlic salt
1 teaspoon salt
1 teaspoon pepper
2 to 4 tablespoons butter

MEATBALLS: Combine the ground beef, ground pork, water chestnuts, garlic, oats, milk, Worcestershire sauce, garlic salt, salt and pepper in a bowl and mix well. Shape into forty-eight small meatballs. Heat some of the butter in a sauté pan. Add the meatballs in batches and cook until brown on all sides, adding additional butter as needed. Drain on paper towels.

1 cup sugar
1/4 cup vinegar
1/4 cup water
1 teaspoon paprika
1/2 teaspoon salt
2 teaspoons cornstarch
1 tablespoon cold water

SWEET-AND-SOUR SAUCE: Combine the sugar, vinegar, 1/4 cup water, the paprika and salt in a skillet or sauté pan. Cook for 5 minutes, stirring occasionally. Blend the cornstarch with 1 tablespoon cold water in a cup. Add to the hot mixture and cook until thickened, stirring constantly; do not boil, as this may cause the sauce to break.

TO SERVE: Place the meatballs in a chafing dish and add the sauce, mixing gently to coat well.

Scallops and Oysters in Spinach Cream Sauce

Serves 6 to 8

*Part of the fun in creating food is making the presentation
unique. To accomplish this here, I have suggested making pastry scallop
shells out of phyllo dough. They are then used to decorate
the final dish, making it quite glamorous.*

1 package phyllo dough
1/2 cup (1 stick) butter, melted
Scallop shells

PHYLLO SCALLOP SHELLS: Cut the phyllo sheets into halves and cover with a damp kitchen towel. Brush half of one sheet at a time with butter and fold the sheet over. Press it into a scallop shell and cut or tear off the edges. Place a second scallop shell on top and press down firmly. Repeat with the remaining pastry and place on a baking sheet. Bake at 350 degrees for 5 to 10 minutes or until brown. Remove from the scallop shells and store in an airtight container.

1/4 cup (1/2 stick) butter
2 tablespoons chopped
    green onions
1/4 cup all-purpose flour
1 cup clam juice
1 cup half-and-half
1 bunch fresh spinach,
    coarsely chopped
Salt, freshly ground black
    pepper and cayenne pepper
    to taste
1 pound scallops, thinly sliced,
    and/or drained oysters

SCALLOPS AND OYSTERS IN SPINACH CREAM SAUCE: Melt the butter in a saucepan and add the green onions. Sauté for 5 minutes or until tender. Stir in the flour and cook for 1 to 2 minutes. Add the clam juice and half-and-half. Cook over medium-high heat until very thick, stirring constantly. Add the spinach and season with salt, black pepper and cayenne pepper. Purée the mixture in a food processor and return to the saucepan. Add the scallops and/or oysters and cook for 3 minutes or just until cooked through.

Chopped roasted red
    bell pepper

TO FINISH AND SERVE: Spoon the seafood in spinach mixture into individual ramekins and top with roasted red bell pepper. Bake at 350 degrees for 10 minutes or until bubbly. Top each with two phyllo scallop shells back to back.

VARIATION: To simplify the recipe, fill the natural scallop shells with the scallop mixture instead of using ramekins, and omit the pastry shells.

CHARRED SHRIMP WITH RED GINGER BARBECUE SAUCE ON ARUGULA SALAD

SERVES 4 TO 6

The charred shrimp in this recipe is sure to bcome a favorite.
Serve it alone or in a salad as suggested here.

---

1 teaspoon minced garlic
1 tablespoon peanut oil
1 teaspoon minced ginger
1 bunch scallions, chopped
2 tablespoons dark brown sugar
4 teaspoons dark soy sauce
2 teaspoons sherry vinegar
1 tablespoon sherry
3 tablespoons tomato sauce
1 teaspoon sriracha hot sauce
1 teaspoon cornstarch
2 teaspoons sherry

RED GINGER BARBECUE SAUCE: Sauté the garlic in the peanut oil in a stainless steel saucepan until tender. Add the ginger and scallions and sauté until the scallions are translucent. Stir in the brown sugar, soy sauce, vinegar and 2 teaspoons sherry. Cook until of the desired consistency. Add the tomato sauce and hot sauce and simmer for 1 minute. Dissolve the cornstarch in 2 teaspoons sherry in a cup and add to the hot mixture. Cook until thickened, stirring constantly. Store, covered, in the refrigerator for up to 4 days.

---

2 tablespoons soy sauce
2 tablespoons sesame oil
2 tablespoons olive oil
2 teaspoons sugar

SESAME SOY SALAD DRESSING: Combine the soy sauce, sesame oil, olive oil and sugar in a mini-food processor and process until smooth.
‘

---

1 1/2 tablespoons peanut oil
1 pound (16- to 20-count) shrimp, peeled

CHARRED SHRIMP: Heat a wok over high heat for 3 minutes. Add 1/2 tablespoon of the peanut oil and one-third of the shrimp at a time. Cook the shrimp for 4 to 5 minutes or until charred, shaking the wok occasionally. Remove with a slotted spoon and repeat with the remaining peanut oil and shrimp. Return all the shrimp to the wok.

---

1 scallion, chopped
1 to 2 bunches arugula
1/3 cup toasted sesame seeds

TO FINISH AND SERVE: Add the red ginger barbecue sauce and the chopped scallion to the shrimp in the wok and stir-fry for 30 to 60 seconds. Place the arugula on a serving platter and top with the sesame soy salad dressing and the sesame seeds. Arrange the shrimp decoratively around the salad.

NOTE For individual salads, consider making napoleons from fried won tons layered with shrimp and salad.

POTATO LATKES WITH APPLESAUCE AND SOUR CREAM

SERVES 10 TO 12

*Serving latkes is a tradition at many Hanukkah celebrations,
although I think you will find these potato pancakes great at any time of
the year. They are usually served with applesauce and sour cream.*

4 medium baking potatoes
2 eggs
1 small onion, grated
1/4 cup all-purpose flour
1 teaspoon salt
1/2 teaspoon pepper
1/4 cup (or more) vegetable oil

POTATO LATKES: Peel and grate the potatoes. Place in enough ice water to cover in a bowl and let stand for 1 hour. Drain well and squeeze out any excess water. Beat the eggs lightly in a bowl. Add the potatoes, onion, flour, salt and pepper; mix well.

Heat the vegetable oil in a sauté pan. Drop the potato mixture by large tablespoonfuls into the pan. Sauté until brown on both sides, pressing down with a spatula to flatten and adding additional oil as needed.

Applesauce
Sour cream

TO SERVE: Place the latkes on serving plates and top with applesauce and sour cream to serve immediately or reheat in a 400-degree oven for 10 to 12 minutes to serve later.

NOTE: There are many good mixes for potato latkes on the market. If you do use a mix, add 1 1/2 cups of grated potatoes for each six ounces of mix.

Ricotta Corn Cakes with Mushroom Salsa

Makes 24 to 30

These small corn cakes are a wonderful base for many toppings. Simple change the size of the corn cakes, and the dish becomes either a first course or a light lunch. Serve them alone with butter or syrup for brunch.

1/4 cup (1/2 stick) butter
4 scallions with some of the
   tops, finely chopped
4 eggs
1 cup ricotta cheese
1/3 cup all-purpose flour
1/3 cup yellow cornmeal
1/2 teaspoon salt
1 cup frozen corn, thawed
Butter

CORN CAKES: Melt 1/4 cup butter in a small sauté pan. Add the scallions and sauté until tender; cool to room temperature. Combine with the eggs, ricotta cheese, flour, cornmeal and salt in a food processor and process until smooth, scraping down the side of the bowl as needed. Spoon into a bowl and stir in the corn.

Add a small amount of butter and 1 tablespoon corn cake batter at a time to a nonstick skillet. Cook until the cake appears dry on the top. Turn the cake over and cook for 30 seconds longer. Remove to a platter and repeat with the remaining batter.

2 to 3 tablespoons olive oil
2 garlic cloves, minced
1 cup minced onion
1 pound mushrooms, chopped
3 Roma tomatoes, chopped
1/2 cup chopped fresh basil
1 teaspoon salt
2 to 3 tablespoons
   chopped parsley

MUSHROOM SALSA: Heat the olive oil in a sauté pan. Add the garlic and onion and sauté until translucent. Add the mushrooms, tomatoes, basil and salt. Cook until most of the liquid has evaporated. Stir in the parsley.

Sour cream
Chopped tomato

TO FINISH AND SERVE: Reheat the corn cakes on a baking sheet in a 350-degree oven. Spread with sour cream and top with the mushroom salsa. Sprinkle with chopped tomato.

PASTA WITH GRILLED CHICKEN, WILD MUSHROOMS AND HAM

SERVES 4

*This dish is actually low in fat, but that is not
its main appeal. It is a great light lunch or dinner as well as
a first course and a staple in my household.*

3 boneless skinless
   chicken breasts
2 tablespoons olive oil
8 ounces button mushrooms or
   wild mushrooms, sliced
2 garlic cloves, chopped
6 slices smoked ham or low-fat
   smoked ham, chopped
4 green onions, chopped
Chicken stock (optional)
1 tablespoon cornstarch
1 to 2 cups evaporated
   skim milk
1 tablespoon beef extract
Nutmeg, salt and pepper
   to taste
Cooked fettucine

PASTA: Spray a grill pan with nonstick cooking spray and add the chicken. Grill on both sides until cooked through. Remove the chicken and slice.

    Heat the olive oil in a 3-quart saucepan. Add the mushrooms and garlic and sauté until the mushrooms are tender. Add the ham and green onions. Sauté until heated through, moistening with chicken stock to prevent sticking if needed. Blend the cornstarch with 2 tablespoons of the evaporated milk in a cup. Add the remaining evaporated milk to the mushroom mixture and stir in the cornstarch mixture. Bring to a boil and cook until thickened, stirring constantly. Stir in the beef extract and season with nutmeg, salt and pepper. Add the chicken and pasta and cook until heated through.

1/4 cup chopped chives
Grated Parmigiano-Reggiano
   cheese

TO SERVE: Spoon the chicken and pasta onto serving plates and top with the chives and cheese.

KATIE'S CEVICHE

MAKES 8 CUPS

My father, John H. Wood, was born near Rockport, Texas.
This gulf coast town remains important to me, for my paternal relatives
and both my parents are buried in its small cemetery. My earliest
memories are of summers spent fishing or crabbing there in canals and
on the shores. My mother, Katie, became quite proficient at finding
many ways to prepare our catch. Ceviche is one of her all-time greats.

10 fillets of fresh trout, skinned
   (about 2¹/2 pounds)
1¹/2 to 2 cups fresh lime juice
4 tomatoes, peeled and
   finely chopped
3 green bell peppers,
   finely chopped
2 small hot chiles,
   finely chopped
2 onions, finely chopped
¹/4 cup chopped parsley
1 teaspoon oregano
¹/2 teaspoon ground cloves
1 tablespoon salt
2 tablespoons olive oil
Tabasco sauce to taste

CEVICHE: Cut the trout fillets into bite-size pieces. Combine with the lime juice in a shallow dish, coating well. Marinate in the refrigerator for 4 to 5 hours; drain and pat dry with paper towels. Combine the fish with the tomatoes, green bell peppers, hot chiles, onions, parsley, oregano, ground cloves and salt in a bowl. Add the olive oil and Tabasco sauce and toss to mix well. Chill for 5 hours or longer.

Crackers or toasted tortillas
Lettuce cups
Lime wedges

TO SERVE: Spoon into a large bowl and serve with crackers to serve as an appetizer. To serve as a first course, spoon into lettuce cups and serve with a wedge of lime and crackers.

QUICHE LORRAINE AUX POIREAUX

SERVES 6 TO 8

A quiche is definitely classic French cuisine, one of those basic recipes that never goes out of style. This leek quiche with bacon can serve as the basis for many creative dishes.

2¹/₂ cups all-purpose flour
1 cup (2 sticks)
  butter, chopped
Salt to taste
²/₃ cup water

BASIC PÂTE BRISÉE: Combine the flour, butter and salt in a food processor and process until the mixture resembles small peas. Add the water and process until the mixture comes together. Knead lightly on a floured surface and chill if necessary to firm up. Roll on a lightly floured surface and fit into a quiche pan. Line with foil and weight with beans or uncooked rice. Bake at 400 degrees for 10 to 12 minutes. Remove the weights and foil and pull the side up if it shows signs of shrinkage. Bake for 5 minutes longer.

2 tablespoons butter
4 leeks, cut into halves
  lengthwise, cleaned
  and chopped
Salt and pepper to taste
6 slices bacon, crisp-fried
  and crumbled
¹/₂ cup (2 ounces) grated
  Parmesan cheese
3 eggs
1 tablespoon Dijon mustard
  or pommery mustard
1³/₄ cups light cream or
  heavy cream
Shredded Swiss cheese
1 tablespoon finely
  chopped parsley

QUICHE: Melt the butter in a heavy sauté pan and add the leeks. Sauté for 5 minutes, stirring constantly. Season with salt and pepper. Spread in the pâte brisée and sprinkle with the bacon and Parmesan cheese.

Combine the eggs and Dijon mustard in a blender and process for 2 seconds. Add the cream and process until smooth. Pour over the leek mixture and sprinkle with Swiss cheese and parsley. Bake at 350 degrees for 30 to 40 minutes or until a knife inserted into the center comes out clean. Cut into wedges.

SWISS CHEESE SOUFFLÉ

SERVES 6

*Making a soufflé requires a classic technique that everyone
should know. It is a good company dish because most of the preparation
can be done in advance. Only the beaten egg whites
need to be added just before baking. I love to serve it at lunch
with a green salad and bread.*

Shredded Swiss cheese or
   Parmesan cheese
6 tablespoons butter
7 tablespoons all-purpose flour
2 cups milk
6 egg yolks
1 tablespoon Dijon mustard
Grated nutmeg to taste
Salt and pepper to taste
1½ cups (6 ounces) shredded
   Swiss cheese
7 egg whites
½ cup (2 ounces) shredded
   Swiss cheese

Double a sheet of foil and wrap it tightly around a 6-cup soufflé dish that is 7 inches in diameter; the foil should form a collar that extends above the rim of the dish. Secure the foil with kitchen twine or a rubber band. Oil the dish and foil collar or spray with nonstick cooking spray and sprinkle lightly with Swiss cheese or Parmesan cheese.

Melt the butter in a 1- to 2-quart saucepan. Stir in the flour and cook over low heat for 2 to 3 minutes or until the flour is incorporated. Add the milk and cook over medium heat until very thick, whisking constantly. Whisk the egg yolks into the mixture one at a time. Whisk in the Dijon mustard, nutmeg, salt and pepper. Add 1½ cups Swiss cheese and heat until the cheese melts, whisking constantly.

Beat the egg whites in a bowl until stiff but not dry. Fold into the warm mixture one-half at a time. Fold in ½ cup Swiss cheese. Spoon into the prepared soufflé dish. Run a knife around the edge of the dish and foil, then in a circle 1 inch from the edge to form the crown when baked. Bake at 400 degrees for 25 to 30 minutes. Remove the foil collar and serve immediately.

Soups and Salads

Wheat Berry Salad with Blue Cheese and Edamame
(recipe on page 75)

Golden Gazpacho with Shrimp Salsa

The yellow tomatoes used in this wonderfully fresh dish are usually only available in the summer. The addition of the shrimp in the salsa makes it quite glamorous, but it is also good without the seafood.

1 pound yellow tomatoes,
    cut into quarters and seeded
    (about 3 tomatoes)
1 small cucumber, peeled,
    seeded and cut into
    1-inch pieces
2 yellow bell peppers, seeded
    and cut into 1-inch pieces
1 jalapeño chile, seeded
1 cup vegetable broth
2 tablespoons white
    wine vinegar
1 teaspoon salt
Pepper to taste

GAZPACHO: Combine the tomatoes, cucumber, yellow bell peppers and jalapeño chile with the vegetable broth, vinegar and salt in a blender; process until puréed. Strain into a bowl and season with pepper. Chill, covered, for 8 hours or until very cold.

Celery, lemon slices, onion,
    oregano, thyme and salt to
    season the shrimp
6 ounces peeled medium
    shrimp or crab meat
1 red tomato, seeded and diced
1/2 small red onion, diced
1/2 yellow bell pepper, diced
1/2 red bell pepper, diced
2 teaspoons fresh lime juice
Salt and pepper to taste

SHRIMP SALSA: Season a saucepan of water with the celery, lemon, onion, oregano, thyme and salt. Bring to a boil and add the shrimp; cook just until pink and tender. Drain the shrimp and cut into 1/4-inch pieces. Combine the tomato, onion, yellow bell pepper, red bell pepper and lime juice in a bowl. Season with salt and pepper and mix well. Add the shrimp and toss to mix.

TO SERVE: Spoon the salsa into a mound in the centers of chilled soup bowls. Ladle the gazpacho around the salsa.

Golden Gazpacho with Shrimp Salsa

Cold Cream of Cauliflower Soup with Caviar

Serves 8 to 10

There is nothing more dramatic than white and black together.
This cold white soup topped with black caviar is spectacular in both
appearance and taste. If caviar is not to your taste, use the
white soup as the backdrop for any colorful garnish, such as swirls
of basil oil or chopped chives.

---

2 to 3 tablespoons olive oil
1 small onion, chopped
1 potato, chopped
1 small head cauliflower, cut
  into 1-inch florets
6 to 8 cups chicken broth
1/2 to 1 cup half-and-half
Salt to taste

Soup: Heat the olive oil in a 3-quart saucepan. Add the onion and sweat, covered, over medium heat for 3 to 4 minutes or until tender, stirring occasionally. Add the potato, cauliflower and enough chicken broth to cover. Simmer, covered, for 7 to 10 minutes or until the vegetables are tender. Pour into a metal bowl placed in a larger bowl of ice and let stand until cool. Process in two batches in a blender until very smooth. Combine with the half-and-half in a bowl and season with salt.

---

3 tablespoons whipping cream,
  lightly whipped
1/4 cup black caviar
Chopped chives or sorrel
  (optional)

To Serve: Ladle the soup into eight shallow bowls. Top with a dollop of whipped cream and about 1 1/2 teaspoon of caviar. Add chopped chives or sorrel.

Note: Less expensive brands of caviar should be rinsed before using. Remember that cold soups require more salt than hot soups.

DUO OF CREAMY CARROT SOUP AND WHITE BEAN SOUP

SERVES 6 TO 8

*I love the idea of serving two compatible soups in one bowl.
Since the carrot soup is thickened with white beans, these two soups are
a natural combination. Instead of just pouring two soups into one
bowl, I use the technique of serving the orange carrot soup in a circle
around the white bean soup. I served it for thirty people at
Christmas with the help of my wonderful nieces.*

2 tablespoons olive oil
1/2 onion, chopped
1 rib celery, chopped
2 or 3 garlic cloves, chopped
1 teaspoon chopped fresh thyme
2 (15-ounce) cans Great
    Northern beans, drained
1 1/2 (15-ounce) cans
    chicken broth
1/2 cup heavy cream

WHITE BEAN SOUP: Heat the olive oil in a saucepan and add the onion, celery, garlic and thyme. Sauté over low heat until the onion is translucent. Add the beans, chicken broth and cream. Cook for 45 minutes or until the vegetables are tender. Process the mixture in a blender until smooth, adding additional chicken broth if needed for the desired consistency. Heat to serving temperature and keep warm.

5 large carrots, peeled and cut
    into 1/2-inch pieces
1 large onion, cut into quarters
1 large bay leaf
1 1/4 teaspoons chopped
    fresh thyme
1/4 teaspoon ground allspice
2 (15-ounce) cans reduced-
    sodium chicken broth
1/2 to 1 (15-ounce) can Great
    Northern beans, drained
1/2 cup heavy cream or milk
    (optional)

CARROT SOUP: Combine the carrots, onion, bay leaf, thyme and allspice with the chicken broth in a large saucepan and bring to a boil. Reduce the heat and simmer, covered, for 15 minutes or until the carrots are tender. Discard the bay leaf. Add the white beans and cream and cook until heated through. Process the mixture in a food processor until smooth. Return to the saucepan and add additional chicken broth if needed for the desired consistency. Heat to serving temperature and keep warm.

Chopped chives

TO ASSEMBLE AND SERVE: Place a round cutter or mold in the center of each soup bowl. Pour the white bean soup into the ring mold and pour the carrot soup around the outer edge of the mold. Remove the mold carefully and sprinkle with chives.

CREAM OF MUSHROOM SOUP WITH PASTRY DOME

SERVES 6 TO 8

I have dressed up a basic cream of mushroom soup recipe by serving it in ovenproof bowls topped with commercially available puff pastry. It makes for a spectacular presentation.

1/4 cup (1/2 stick) butter
1/2 onion, chopped
2 garlic cloves, minced
2 pounds button
   mushrooms and/or
   wild mushrooms, sliced
1 teaspoon dried thyme
1/4 cup all-purpose flour
3 cups (or more) beef stock
1 cup light cream
1/3 cup dry sherry
Salt and pepper to taste

CREAM OF MUSHROOM SOUP: Melt the butter in a 3-quart saucepan and add the onion and garlic. Sauté until the vegetables are tender. Add the mushrooms and thyme and sauté until the mushrooms are tender. Add the flour and cook for 1 to 2 minutes, stirring constantly. Add the beef stock all at once and cook over medium-high heat until thickened, stirring frequently. Stir in the cream and add additional beef stock if needed for the desired consistency. Season with sherry, salt and pepper. Ladle into individual ovenproof bowls.

Frozen puff pastry, thawed
1 egg
1 tablespoon water

TO FINISH AND SERVE: Roll the puff pastry thin on a lightly floured surface and cut into circles the size of the tops of the soup bowls. Place the circles on the soup and press to the bowl to seal. Brush with a mixture of the egg and water. Bake at 350 degrees for 20 to 25 minutes or until puffed and brown. Serve immediately.

NOTE: You can assemble this dish several days in advance and store in the refrigerator until time to bake. Cover the pastry well to keep it from drying out.

GREEN PEA SOUP WITH LEMON CREAM

Recipes that call for green peas are usually best prepared in the spring when fresh peas are available. This recipe, however, uses frozen peas, making it a good dish to serve at any time. Its bright green color and fresh taste make it memorable.

1¹/₂ cups sour cream
1 tablespoon lemon juice
Salt to taste

LEMON CREAM: Combine the sour cream, lemon juice and salt in a blender or mini-food processor and process until smooth. Pour into a squeeze bottle and store in the refrigerator.

---

2 slices very thin Pepperidge
  Farm bread
2 tablespoons butter
1 tablespoon minced
  fresh rosemary

ROSEMARY CROUTONS: Cut the bread into ¹/₂-inch cubes. Sprinkle on a baking sheet and toast at 250 degrees for 30 minutes or until crisp. Heat the butter in a sauté pan. Add the bread cubes and rosemary and sauté until golden brown. Cool to room temperature and store in an airtight container.

---

2 tablespoons olive oil
1 cup chopped leeks
1 cup chopped green onions
1 cup chopped celery
1 sprig rosemary
¹/₂ cup parsley leaves
1 (16-ounce) package frozen
  green peas, thawed
4 (15-ounce) cans chicken
  broth, heated
Salt and pepper to taste

GREEN PEA SOUP: Heat the olive oil in a saucepan. Add the leeks, green onions, celery and rosemary. Sweat, covered, over low heat for 10 to 15 minutes or until tender but not brown. Add the parsley, peas and chicken broth. Bring to a boil and cook for several minutes. Pour into a bowl and then place in a larger bowl of ice water. Discard the rosemary and stir the soup to cool and preserve its green color.

Remove and reserve 2 cups of the liquid. Process the remaining soup in a blender until puréed, adding as much of the reserved liquid as needed for the desired consistency. Season with salt and pepper and store in the refrigerator.

---

4 ounces frozen peas, thawed
4 slices bacon, crisp-fried
  and crumbled

TO ASSEMBLE AND SERVE: Ladle the soup into bowls and stir in the peas. Squeeze the lemon cream in a decorative swirl on the top and sprinkle the croutons and crumbled bacon in the center.

POBLANO SOUP WITH CORN AND AVOCADO

SERVES 4 TO 6

Poblano soup is a traditional Southwestern soup. The only concern when preparing it is the varying degree of heat produced by the poblanos, which grow milder as they become older and darker. Be sure to remove all seeds and veins to reduce the risk that the soup will be too spicy.

2 poblano chiles
2 tablespoons olive oil
1 onion, chopped
2 garlic cloves, chopped
2 tablespoons butter
2 tablespoons all-purpose flour
2 cups (or more) chicken broth
1 cup heavy cream
1 large potato, chopped
Salt and pepper to taste
1 potato, cut into small cubes
1 (8-ounce) package
    frozen corn
1/2 cup minced fresh cilantro

SOUP: Place the poblano chiles on a baking sheet and broil until roasted and charred on all sides. Peel and seed the chiles.

Heat the olive oil in a saucepan. Add the onion and garlic and sauté for 5 minutes or until tender. Melt the butter in the same saucepan and stir in the flour. Cook for 1 to 2 minutes or until the flour is incorporated completely, stirring constantly. Add the chicken broth, cream and 1 large potato. Cook over medium-high heat until thickened, stirring constantly. Stir in the roasted chiles and season with salt and pepper. Cook until the potato is tender.

Process the soup in a blender until smooth, adding additional chicken broth if needed for the desired consistency. Adjust the seasoning. Return the soup to the saucepan and add the remaining potato and corn. Simmer until the potato is tender. Stir in the cilantro.

Shredded Monterey Jack cheese
Diced avocado
Fried tortilla strips

TO SERVE: Ladle the soup into soup bowls and sprinkle generously with Monterey Jack cheese. Top with avocado and fried tortilla strips. Serve hot.

NOTE: The best fried tortilla strips are homemade. Cut commercial tortillas into strips and fry in 2 to 3 cups of heated vegetable oil for 2 to 3 minutes or until crisp. Drain on paper towels and season with salt while hot.

RED PEPPER GAZPACHO WITH AVOCADO AND LOBSTER

SERVES 4

*Before going to Le Manoir cooking school in 2001, my assistant
Sally Helland and I hosted a farewell dinner. I was looking for something
with an English flavor to serve and found this, from Restaurant
Mirabelle, in a cookbook I bought when I was last in London. You will
find this "no cook" soup extremely refreshing and elegant.*

1¹/2 to 2 red bell peppers,
    seeded and chopped
3 plum tomatoes
¹/2 medium onion, chopped
¹/2 cucumber, peeled, seeded
    and coarsely chopped
3 or 4 garlic cloves, chopped
¹/3 cup sherry vinegar
³/4 to 1 cup chicken broth
Tabasco sauce to taste
Salt and pepper to taste

RED PEPPER GAZPACHO: Combine the red bell peppers, tomatoes, onion, cucumber and garlic with the vinegar and chicken broth in a food processor. Process until smooth. Press the mixture through a sieve into a bowl and season with Tabasco sauce, salt and pepper. Chill in the refrigerator.

Onion, celery, bay leaf and salt
    to season the lobster
Lobster tails

LOBSTER: Season a large saucepan of water with onion, celery, bay leaf and salt and bring to a boil. Add the lobster tails and cook for 2 to 3 minutes or until cooked through; do not overcook. Drain the lobster tails and split down the center back. Remove the meat from the shells and cut into serving pieces, discarding the shells. Store in the refrigerator until needed.

Avocado
Minced onion
Lime juice
Salt and pepper to taste
Chopped chervil, Italian
    parsley or cilantro

TO ASSEMBLE AND SERVE: Mash the avocado with a small amount of minced onion in a bowl. Add lime juice, salt and pepper and mix well. Ladle the gazpacho into bowls and place a large piece of lobster and a dollop of the avocado mixture in each bowl. Garnish with chervil, Italian parsley or cilantro.

NOTE: If you prepare the gazpacho a day in advance, it will separate. Just stir to mix well and it will come back together.

Asparagus Soup with Morel Custard

Serves 8

*It is a contemporary idea to garnish a soup with a dollop of
vegetable custard chosen to complement the soup.*

---

4 ounces morels, coarsely
   chopped, or 4 ounces dried
   morels with 4 ounces fresh
   shiitake mushrooms
2 tablespoons olive oil
3/4 cup minced onion
Salt and pepper to taste
1 cup heavy cream
2 egg yolks
1 egg

MOREL CUSTARD: Soak the dried morels in hot water in
a bowl; drain. Heat the olive oil in a medium skillet and
add the morels, onion, salt and pepper. Sauté for 3 to
5 minutes or until the morels begin to release their juices.
Add the cream and bring to a simmer. Simmer for
10 minutes. Season with salt and pepper. Cool to room
temperature. Beat the egg yolks and egg in a bowl.
Add to the cooled mushroom mixture.

    Spoon the mixture into eight buttered 2-ounce
ramekins. Place in a larger baking pan and set on the
center oven rack. Add enough boiling water to reach
halfway up the sides of the ramekins. Cover with foil
and bake at 325 degrees for 20 to 25 minutes or until
the custards are set. Cool slightly.

---

6 pounds asparagus spears
1 tablespoon olive oil
6 to 8 cups chicken broth
1 tablespoon olive oil
2 shallots, minced
1 1/2 cups chopped leeks,
   white portions only
1 cup chopped onion
Kosher salt and freshly ground
   pepper to taste
1/4 cup heavy cream

ASPARAGUS SOUP: Cut the tips from the asparagus
spears and reserve; cut the stems into halves. Sauté the
asparagus stems in 1 tablespoon olive oil in a saucepan
over medium heat for 5 to 10 minutes. Add the chicken
broth and bring to a boil. Reduce the heat and simmer
for 15 minutes. Drain and reserve the cooking liquid.
Discard the asparagus stems.

    Heat 1 tablespoon olive oil in a saucepan over
medium heat. Add the shallots, leeks, onion, kosher
salt and pepper. Sauté for 1 to 2 minutes; do not brown.
Add the reserved asparagus tips. Sauté for 5 minutes
or until the asparagus tips are bright green. Add the
reserved cooking liquid. Simmer for 10 minutes or
until the asparagus is tender, but still bright green.
Stir in the cream. Process the soup in a blender.
Return the soup to the saucepan and adjust the
seasonings. Heat to serving temperature.

Chopped fresh herbs

TO ASSEMBLE AND SERVE: Loosen the custards from the
ramekins with a knife and unmold into eight shallow
soup bowls. Ladle the soup into the bowls and garnish
with fresh herbs. Serve immediately.

LEEK AND POTATO SOUP WITH STILTON CHEESE

SERVES 6 TO 8

This is a traditional vichyssoise enhanced by the addition of Stilton cheese. With this addition, you serve the soup hot rather than cold. To serve it cold, leave out the cheese, sage, and pepper and top it with chopped chives. For a holiday soup, add sautéed red bell pepper and tiny star croutons.

6 tablespoons butter
3 cups chopped leeks, white portions only
1 cup chopped onion
1/2 cup chopped celery (about 2 ribs)
6 cups peeled and chopped potatoes (about 3 to 4 large potatoes)
3 garlic cloves, chopped
2 tablespoons minced fresh sage
4 to 6 cups chicken broth
1 1/2 cups heavy cream
1 to 2 cups chicken broth
Salt and pepper to taste

SOUP: Melt the butter in a large saucepan. Add the leeks, onion, celery, potatoes, garlic and sage. Cover with parchment and cook for 15 minutes or until the leeks, onion and celery are tender. Add 4 cups of the chicken broth and simmer for 15 minutes or until the potatoes are tender. Combine the mixture with the cream in a blender and process until smooth, adding 1 to 2 cups additional chicken broth if needed for the desired consistency. Season with salt and pepper. Return to the saucepan and heat to serving temperature.

1/4 cup port
1/4 cup crumbled Stilton cheese
Minced fresh sage

TO FINISH AND SERVE: Stir the port into the soup just before serving and ladle into soup bowls. Top with the Stilton cheese and fresh sage.

CREAM OF TOMATO AND CARROT SOUP

SERVES 6 TO 8

*The combination of red tomatoes and orange carrots gives
this soup a lovely color, one that would be appropriate for a Valentine's
celebration. We are allowed to become a little tacky on this special
day, so go ahead and add heart-shaped croutons.*

2 tablespoons butter
3 cups chopped carrots
1 onion, chopped
2 garlic cloves, minced
1/4 cup (1/2 stick) butter
1/4 cup all-purpose flour
1 (24-ounce) can tomatoes
1 teaspoon chopped fresh
   dill weed
2 to 3 (or more) cups
   chicken broth
1/2 cup (or more) light cream
Salt and pepper to taste

SOUP: Melt 2 tablespoons butter in a saucepan and
add the carrots, onion and garlic. Sweat the vegetables,
covered, for 10 minutes. Add 1/4 cup butter and
stir in the flour. Cook until the flour is completely
incorporated, stirring constantly. Add the undrained
tomatoes and dill weed. Cook until heated and then
add the chicken broth and cream. Cook until the
mixture thickens and the carrots are tender, stirring
constantly. Process the mixture in a blender until
smooth, adding additional cream or chicken broth if
needed for the desired consistency. Season with salt
and pepper. Return to the saucepan and cook until
heated through or chill in the refrigerator to serve cold.

Sour cream
1 tablespoon milk
Fresh dill weed

TO ASSEMBLE AND SERVE: Combine sour cream with
the milk and dill weed in a mini-food processor and
process until smooth. Spoon into a squeeze bottle.
Ladle the soup into bowls and pipe a heart or other
shape onto the top with the sour cream mixture.

ICED CREAM OF TOMATO SOUP

SERVES 4 TO 6

This soup is great for our hot Texas summers. It is refreshing and pretty, but best of all, it is best served cold. Be sure to leave it chunky when you process it for the best results.

6 tomatoes, about 2 pounds
1 tablespoon butter
1 onion, coarsely chopped
1 tablespoon tomato paste
1 cup chicken broth
$^1/_2$ teaspoon sugar
$^1/_2$ teaspoon dried thyme
$^1/_2$ teaspoon salt
$^3/_4$ cup heavy cream
$^1/_4$ cup sour cream
$^1/_4$ cup lime juice
Salt and pepper to taste

SOUP: Drop the tomatoes in a saucepan of boiling water for 45 to 60 seconds. Remove with a slotted spoon and refresh in cold water. Slip the peels off easily and seed and chop the tomatoes.

Melt the butter in a saucepan and add the onion. Cover with a buttered round of waxed paper and the lid and sweat over low heat for 15 minutes or until tender. Add the tomatoes, tomato paste, chicken broth, sugar, thyme and salt. Simmer, covered, for 10 minutes. Cool to room temperature. Combine with the heavy cream, sour cream, lime juice, salt and pepper in a food processor. Process just until coarsely chopped. Chill in the refrigerator.

4 to 6 lime slices
4 to 6 sprigs parsley

TO SERVE: Ladle into soup bowls and garnish with a slice of lime and a sprig of parsley.

Senegalese Soup

*Senegalese soup is an old family recipe. It became part of my life when
I was very young, and I served it at the christening luncheon of
my first child, Ramona. Even after all these years, it remains dear to my
heart. Isn't it wonderful that food served on special occasions
can trigger such wonderful memories?*

**Carrot, celery, parsley, bay
leaf, thyme, marjoram, salt
and pepper to season the
chicken broth**
1 whole chicken
4 egg yolks
2 cups heavy cream
2 teaspoons curry powder
**Cayenne pepper, salt and
pepper to taste**

Soup: Season a saucepan of water with carrot, celery, parsley, bay leaf, thyme, marjoram, salt and pepper. Add the chicken and cook until tender. Remove the chicken; strain and reserve the broth. Cut the chicken into bite-size pieces and measure 2 to 3 cups for the soup; discard the skin and bones. Store in the refrigerator.

Heat the reserved chicken broth in a large saucepan. Combine the egg yolks, cream, curry powder and cayenne pepper in a bowl. Stir a small amount of the hot broth into the egg yolk mixture; stir the egg yolk mixture gradually into the hot broth. Cook until slightly thickened, stirring constantly. Cool the soup to room temperature and season with salt and pepper. Chill in the refrigerator.

Chopped parsley

To Assemble and Serve: Combine the chopped chicken and the soup base. Serve cold with chopped parsley.

ROASTED GARLIC AND PROSCIUTTO SOUP WITH GRUYÈRE CHEESE

SERVES 6 TO 8

This is a great basic soup that can be changed in endless ways. In San Francisco, it was served as garlic soup with a garnish of fried leeks and baby shrimp. In another restaurant, the soup was presented with slivers of fried garlic. Sautéed frog legs were served as a side dish to be eaten along with the soup. Use your own creativity.

2 whole garlic bulbs
Olive oil
1 onion, chopped or
   2 leeks, chopped
2 tablespoons vegetable oil
1/2 cup white wine
4 russet potatoes, peeled and
   cut into 2-inch pieces
6 to 8 cups (or more)
   chicken broth
Salt and pepper to taste
2 tablespoons dry sherry
2 tablespoons Cognac
12 ounces Gruyère cheese,
   shredded

SOUP: Cut the tops off the bulbs of garlic to expose the tops of the cloves. Coat with olive oil and wrap in foil. Roast at 400 degrees for 50 minutes or until very tender.

Sauté the onion in the vegetable oil in a saucepan until tender. Add the white wine and simmer until reduced by one-half. Add the potatoes and chicken broth. Squeeze the garlic out of the skins into the saucepan and mix well. Season with salt and pepper. Cook for 20 minutes or until the potatoes are very tender. Process the mixture in a food processor until smooth, adding additional chicken broth if needed for the desired consistency. Stir in the sherry and cognac and adjust the seasonings. Stir in the Gruyère cheese until melted if serving immediately; store in the refrigerator and reheat to serve later, adding the cheese at serving time.

1 red bell pepper, diced
1 bunch scallions, diced
8 ounces prosciutto, chopped
2 tablespoons butter
Croutons
1/4 cup (1/2 stick) butter

TO FINISH AND SERVE: Sauté the red bell pepper, scallions and prosciutto in 2 tablespoons butter in a sauté pan until tender. Sauté croutons in 1/4 cup butter in a sauté pan. Ladle the soup into soup bowls and top with 1 tablespoon of the prosciutto mixture and a teaspoon of croutons.

NOTE: To make croutons, cut white bread into 1/2-inch cubes and sprinkle on a baking sheet. Dry in a 250-degree oven for 1 hour.

ONION AND FENNEL SOUP WITH SLOW-ROASTED HERBED SALMON

SERVES 4

In the spring of 2006, I took a group to Napa Valley to cook and enjoy the fine wines of the area. We attended a school at Stag's Leap and were once again reminded of the fresh flavors of California cuisine. We were taught a method of slow roasting salmon. It was served on a bed of fava bean purée and also in an onion and fennel soup. I have re-created my version of that recipe here, using this easy method of cooking salmon that turns out moist every time.

1/3 cup olive oil
2 tablespoons butter
1 bunch leeks, white portions only, thinly sliced
1/2 large onion, chopped
1 fennel bulb, white portion only, chopped
3/4 cup white port
2 to 3 (or more) cups chicken broth
Salt and pepper to taste

ONION AND FENNEL SOUP: Heat the olive oil and butter in a large saucepan. Add the leeks, onion and fennel to the saucepan and cover loosely. Sauté over medium-high heat for several minutes, stirring occasionally. Stir in the wine and cook until the vegetables are tender. Combine in a blender with enough chicken broth to make a thick soup and process until smooth. Season with salt and pepper.

---

1 salmon fillet with skin
2 cups olive oil
Salt and pepper to taste
3 cups chopped mixed tarragon, chives, chervil and basil

SLOW-ROASTED HERBED SALMON: Remove any small bones from the salmon. Wash the salmon and cut into pieces 1 1/2 inches thick and coat with some of the olive oil. Season with salt and pepper and press a generous amount of the chopped herbs onto all sides. Place the salmon on a baking sheet coated with the remaining olive oil and top with a lightly oiled piece of baking parchment. Roast at 200 degrees for 25 to 30 minutes or until the thickest portions of the salmon are firm to the touch.

TO SERVE: Reheat the soup and ladle into wide shallow soup bowls. Place one portion of salmon in each bowl and serve immediately.

Oyster Stew

It is amazing that anything this simple can be so good.
If you are an oyster lover, this traditional soup will become a favorite.
I always think of serving oysters at Christmas,
and this is definitely a good choice.

---

1 cup milk
1 1/2 cups light cream
3 tablespoons butter
1/2 teaspoon Worcestershire
   sauce
Tabasco sauce to taste
1/2 teaspoon salt
Freshly ground black pepper
   and cayenne pepper
   to taste
1 pint oysters, shelled, with
   the liquor reserved

STEW: Combine the milk, cream, butter, Worcestershire sauce, Tabasco sauce, salt, black pepper and cayenne pepper in a 3-quart saucepan. Bring to a boil and reduce to a simmer. Add the oysters with the reserved liquor and return to a boil. Remove from the heat immediately.

Paprika
Chopped chives
Oyster crackers (optional)

TO SERVE: Ladle the stew into bowls and sprinkle lightly with paprika and chopped chives. Serve with oyster crackers.

NOTE: *The base of the stew can be prepared in advance, but once you add the oysters to it and return it to a boil, it must be served immediately. This method will cook the oysters perfectly.*

Thai Noodle Soup with Shrimp and Coconut Milk

Serves 4 to 6

*Today our tastes are very influenced by Asia, and this recipe contains
many of the wonderful flavors used in Thai cooking. Don't be
intimidated by the long list of ingredients. Once you have gathered
everything needed, the dish comes together quickly.*

1 small onion, chopped
1 (2-inch) piece fresh
   ginger, peeled
3 garlic cloves, minced
2 or 3 fresh serrano chiles
1 stalk lemon grass, trimmed
1 tablespoon
   ground coriander
1 teaspoon ground cumin
1 teaspoon ground turmeric
1/3 cup fish sauce
2 teaspoons brown sugar
2 tablespoons peanut oil
Shells from 1 pound shrimp
2 cups chicken broth
3 cups water
1 (14-ounce) can
   coconut milk
1/4 cup fresh lime juice
1 teaspoon kosher salt

SOUP BASE: Combine the onion, ginger, garlic, chiles, lemon grass, coriander, cumin, turmeric, fish sauce and brown sugar in a food processor and process into a paste, scraping the side of the bowl as needed.

Heat the peanut oil in a heavy saucepan. Add the paste mixture and sauté for 5 to 10 minutes or until it becomes aromatic and deepens in color, stirring frequently. Stir in the shrimp shells. Sauté for 2 minutes or until the shrimp shells are pink.

Add the chicken broth, water, coconut milk, lime juice and kosher salt; mix well. Bring to a boil and reduce the heat. Simmer for 30 minutes. Strain the broth into a bowl and discard the solids. Return to the saucepan.

6 to 8 ounces Chinese egg
   noodles, cooked
1 cup peeled, chopped and
   seeded English cucumber
1 cup bean sprouts
1 cup snow peas, trimmed
1/2 cup sliced green onions
1 or 2 serrano chiles, sliced
1/2 cup chopped fresh cilantro
1/2 cup chopped fresh basil
1 pound shrimp, peeled
   and cooked

SOUP: Heat the soup base to serving temperature. Add the noodles, cucumber, bean sprouts, snow peas, green onions, chiles, cilantro, basil and shrimp. Ladle into soup bowls and serve immediately.

Sesame Chicken Salad with Radishes

Serves 6

This is a perfect salad for a light lunch or summer supper. It can be individually plated or served on a platter for a buffet. Radishes are avoided by many, but trust me, this salad is a treat.

2 garlic cloves
6 fresh mint leaves, diced
1 (heaping) tablespoon
   Dijon mustard
1/2 cup vinegar
1 teaspoon salt
1 cup olive oil
Pepper to taste

MINT DRESSING: Mince the garlic in a food processor. Add the mint, Dijon mustard, vinegar and salt; pulse until combined. Add the olive oil through the feed tube, processing constantly until smooth. Add the pepper and adjust the seasoning. Store in the refrigerator.

1 tablespoon cumin
1 tablespoon coriander
1/4 cup sesame seeds
6 boneless skinless
   chicken breasts
1/3 cup (or more) olive oil
1 head romaine lettuce,
   cut into strips
2 cups stemmed fresh mint
2 cups thinly sliced
   red radishes

SALAD: Mix the cumin, coriander and sesame seeds in a small bowl. Coat the chicken with the mixture. Heat the olive oil in a sauté pan and add the chicken. Sauté for 3 to 4 minutes on each side or until brown and cooked through, adding additional olive oil if needed. Slice the chicken.

   Combine the romaine lettuce, mint and radishes in a bowl. Add half the mint dressing and toss to coat well.

TO SERVE: Spoon the romaine mixture into the center of individual plates. Fan the chicken slices to one side. Drizzle with additional mint dressing or pass the dressing at the table.

WATERCRESS, SWEET CORN AND BASMATI RICE SALAD

SERVES 4

Besides food, my other passion in life is golf. Last summer this crazy game introduced me to a new friend from Dallas who shares the same two passions. This recipe is a gift from her, and I cannot explain exactly why it is so fantastic. The basmati rice is a must, and regular rice should not be substituted for it. Basmati is an Indian rice and has a better texture if soaked in water for about 20 minutes before cooking.

2 tablespoons red
  wine vinegar
1 tablespoon Dijon mustard
1/2 cup olive oil
Salt and freshly ground
  pepper to taste

RED WINE VINAIGRETTE: Whisk the vinegar and Dijon mustard in a bowl until smooth. Add the olive oil gradually, whisking constantly. Season with salt and pepper. Store in the refrigerator.

1 cup uncooked basmati rice
2 cups water
1/2 teaspoon salt

BASMATI RICE: Soak the rice in enough water to cover in a bowl for 20 minutes; drain. Bring 2 cups water to a boil in a saucepan. Add the rice and salt and return to a boil. Cover and reduce the heat to low. Simmer for 20 minutes or until the water is absorbed. Remove from the heat and let stand for 5 minutes.

2 tablespoons olive oil
1 cup chopped green onions
Kernels from 6 large ears of
  fresh yellow corn
Salt and freshly ground pepper
  to taste
1 1/2 cups toasted pecans,
  coarsely chopped
2 bunches watercress,
  stemmed

SALAD: Heat the olive oil in a large skillet. Add the green onions and sauté for 20 seconds. Add the corn and sauté for 3 minutes or until tender-crisp. Season with salt and pepper. Combine with the rice and pecans in a salad bowl. Add the watercress and red wine vinaigrette. Adjust the seasonings. Serve immediately.

VARIATION: For a main-course salad, add grilled shrimp or sliced grilled chicken or salmon. You can also add chopped tomato for variety and color.

Fresh Mozzarella Salad

Serves 4 to 6

Mozzarella experts believe that this cheese is best eaten when it is the freshest, not aged at all. I enjoyed learning how fresh mozzarella is made, and I am passing it on to you. You will be amazed how easy it is and how wonderful when eaten while still warm.

8 ounces mozzarella curd
1 cup buttermilk
1^1/$_2$ cups water
2 tablespoons kosher salt

FRESH MOZZARELLA: Grate the mozzarella curd into slivers with a grater and place in a glass bowl. Place the buttermilk in a second bowl and keep it close to the curds. Bring the water to a boil in a saucepan. Add the kosher salt and return to a boil. Pour enough of the boiling water over the curd to just cover and let stand for 1 to 2 minutes. Push the curds together gently into the center of the bowl with two wooden spoons. Lift from underneath and hold above the bowl, allowing it to stretch back down into the water. Repeat the process until it appears smooth. Form balls by pulling the desired amount up from the larger mixture and rolling into balls with your hands, smoothing the top; do not overwork the cheese or it will become tough. Place smooth side up in the buttermilk and repeat with the remaining cheese.

4 fresh tomatoes
Fresh basil leaves
Salt and pepper to taste
Olive oil

SALAD: Cut the tomatoes into slices ^{1}/$_4$ inch thick. Slice the fresh mozzarella. Alternate slices of tomato and cheese in overlapping concentric circles on a plate, placing a basil leaf on each cheese slice, half hidden by a tomato slice. Sprinkle with salt and pepper and drizzle with olive oil.

VARIATION: Vary this dish in the summer by using a variety of colored heirloom tomatoes when they are in season.

NOTE: Today, good mozzarella can be found in most high-end markets. If you want to make you own, however, the source for mozzarella curd is Todaro Bros. Specialty Foods, 1-877-472-2767, www.todarobros.com.

CHERRY TOMATO AND FETA SALAD WITH WALNUTS AND BASIL

SERVES 6 TO 8

I am always looking for simple good salads to add to a buffet table.
This combination of ingredients is beautiful in color and delicious in flavor.
The larger the platter on which it is served, the more dramatic the effect.

1 tablespoon chopped shallot
3 tablespoons cider vinegar
1/2 teaspoon honey
Salt and pepper to taste
1/4 cup extra-light olive oil

SHALLOT VINAIGRETTE: Combine the shallot with the vinegar, honey, salt and pepper in a small bowl and whisk to mix well. Add the olive oil gradually, whisking constantly until emulsified. Store in the refrigerator.

6 cups cherry tomatoes
2 cups walnuts
2 cups crumbled feta cheese
1/2 cup coarsely chopped basil
Salt and pepper to taste

SALAD: Cut the cherry tomatoes into halves and place in a bowl. Add the walnuts, feta cheese and basil; toss lightly to mix well. Season with salt and pepper. Chill in the refrigerator.

TO SERVE: Spoon the salad onto a large platter and drizzle with the shallot vinaigrette. Serve cold.

VARIATION: You can add yellow tear-drop tomatoes to this salad when they are in season.

MIXED GREENS WITH MUSHROOMS AND POACHED EGGS

SERVES 6

I choose this salad for my classes both because of its wonderful flavors and because it teaches many basic skills that can be used in other dishes.

1 tablespoon hot
    Dijon mustard
1 garlic clove, chopped
1/4 cup balsamic vinegar
2 tablespoons chopped sage
3/4 cup olive oil
Salt and pepper to taste

BALSAMIC VINAIGRETTE: Combine the Dijon mustard, garlic, balsamic vinegar and sage in a mini-food processor and process until smooth. Add the olive oil gradually through the feed tube, processing constantly until emulsified. Season with salt and pepper.

2 tablespoons butter
4 ounces ham, cut into small
    thick cubes
2 cups corn
1 cup mixed wild mushrooms,
    such as morels or chanterelles
Salt and pepper to taste

VEGETABLES: Melt the butter in a 2-quart saucepan. Add the ham and corn and sauté until light brown. Add the mushrooms and sauté until tender. Season with salt and pepper.

1 tablespoon vinegar
1 tablespoon salt
6 eggs

POACHED EGGS: Fill a wide 3-quart saucepan with water and add the vinegar and salt. Bring to a simmer and break the eggs gently into the water. Poach for 2 minutes or until firm but soft in the center. Remove gently to a bowl of cold water and store in the refrigerator.

2 egg yolks
Juice of 1/2 lemon
1/2 teaspoon salt
1 cup (2 sticks) butter, melted

HOLLANDAISE SAUCE: Combine the eggs, lemon juice and salt in a food processor. Add the hot butter through the feed tube very gradually, processing constantly until smooth. Keep warm.

8 cups mesclun, baby
    watercress or frisée

TO FINISH AND SERVE: Reheat the poached eggs in simmering water for 30 seconds. Reheat the vegetables. Combine the vegetables with the mesclun and vinaigrette in a bowl and toss to mix well. Spoon onto serving plates and top each with a poached egg. Spoon 1 tablespoon Hollandaise sauce onto each egg and serve immediately.

Asian Coleslaw

Serves 5

*Each summer I am fortunate to be invited to spend
time with a dear friend in Rockport, Texas. She is an excellent
cook, and this is a dish I am served on each visit. I would
be truly sad if she ever took it off her menu.*

1/4 cup sesame oil
2 tablespoons vegetable oil
6 tablespoons rice
   wine vinegar
1/4 cup sugar
1 teaspoon salt
1 teaspoon pepper

SESAME VINEGAR DRESSING: Combine the sesame oil, vegetable oil, vinegar, sugar, salt and pepper in a bowl and whisk until smooth.

1/4 cup sliced almonds
3/4 cup sesame seeds
2 tablespoons butter
1 head bok choy, shredded
1 bunch green onions, diced

COLESLAW: Sauté the almonds and sesame seeds in the butter in a sauté pan until brown; drain and cool. Combine with the bok choy and green onions in a bowl. Add the dressing and mix well. Serve immediately.

WHEAT BERRY SALAD
WITH BLUE CHEESE AND EDAMAME

SERVES 6 TO 8

*Wheat berries are whole unprocessed wheat kernels and can
be found in most upscale supermarkets. You can substitute other grains
such as bulgur for them. This salad is extremely useful, as it
can be made in advance and easily transported. It is also beautiful, with
the red cabbage, green spinach, and green edamame. Try it as a light
main dish or as a side dish with grilled meats.*

---

2 tablespoons balsamic vinegar
1 tablespoon Dijon mustard
1/2 cup olive oil
Salt and pepper to taste

BALSAMIC DIJON VINAIGRETTE: Combine the vinegar, Dijon mustard, olive oil, salt and pepper in a small bowl and whisk until smooth.

---

2 cups uncooked
   wheat berries
6 cups water
1 teaspoon salt

WHEAT BERRIES: Combine the wheat berries with the water and salt in a saucepan. Bring to a gentle boil and cook for 30 to 45 minutes or until tender; the water will not have completely evaporated and the grains will be slightly chewy. Drain and cool to room temperature.

---

1 cup thinly sliced
   red cabbage
2 cups julienned spinach
1 cup crumbled blue cheese
2 tomatoes, chopped
1/2 cup chopped green onions
1/2 cucumber, seeded
   and chopped
1 cup chopped red bell pepper
2 to 3 cups frozen shelled
   edamame, thawed, or shelled
   fresh edamame

SALAD: Combine the wheat berries with the cabbage, spinach and blue cheese in a salad bowl. Add the tomatoes, green onions, cucumber, red bell pepper and edamame; toss gently. Add the vinaigrette and toss to coat well. Serve cold or at room temperature.

Meats and Game

Lamb Rack with Provençal Crust (recipe on page 91)

PORK LOIN WITH MAPLE ROOT VEGETABLES

SERVES 6 TO 8

In 1998, I was lucky enough to spend a week at the Greenbrier in West Virginia, which has an outstanding cooking school. They were offering this as one of their featured dishes. I asked for the recipe and have revised it to become my own.

1/2 cup maple syrup
2 tablespoons Dijon mustard

MAPLE DIJON GLAZE: Combine the maple syrup and Dijon mustard in a saucepan. Cook until heated through, stirring to blend well.

---

1 (3-pound) center-cut pork
   loin roast, patted dry
Salt and pepper to taste
1/3 cup Dijon mustard
1 teaspoon dried sage, or
   1/4 cup chopped fresh sage
5 or 6 red potatoes, cut into
   quarters if large
10 small white onions
2 or 3 red bell peppers,
   cut into large pieces
2 cups baby carrots, peeled
Mixed baby vegetables
1/3 cup olive oil
Mixture of chopped fresh
   herbs, such as rosemary,
   thyme, basil, oregano, sage
   and/or garlic

PORK ROAST AND VEGETABLES: Season the pork with salt and pepper. Coat with a mixture of the Dijon mustard and sage. Place in a roasting pan and brush with the maple Dijon glaze. Roast at 400 degrees for 30 minutes.

Combine the potatoes, onions, red bell peppers, carrots and baby vegetables in a bowl. Add the olive oil and fresh herbs; season with salt and pepper and toss to coat well. Arrange around the pork in the roasting pan. Brush the pork and the vegetables with the glaze. Roast for 30 to 60 minutes or to 140 degrees on a meat thermometer that has been inserted into the thickest portion. Reserve 3 tablespoons of the pan drippings for the sauce.

---

1 (16-ounce) can whole
   cranberry sauce
1/4 cup lemon juice

CRANBERRY SAUCE: Combine the 3 tablespoons reserved pan drippings with the cranberry sauce and lemon juice in a small saucepan. Cook over medium heat until the cranberry sauce melts and the mixture is heated through.

Chopped fresh herbs

TO ASSEMBLE AND SERVE: Place the pork on a serving platter and arrange the vegetables around it. Sprinkle with fresh herbs and serve with the cranberry sauce.

Pork Loin with Maple Root Vegetables

PORK WITH VIRGINIA HAM, SPRING VEGETABLES AND FETTUCINE

SERVES 6 TO 8

The Inn at Little Washington, Virginia, is a fantastic stopover in the Washington, D.C. area. Besides being a lovely place to stay, it serves extremely innovative Southern dishes. This recipe is a good example of a one-dish meal that is great for entertaining.

1/4 cup (1/2 stick) butter
2 cups chopped carrots
2 cups chopped celery
2 cups chopped leeks
2 cups chopped onions
8 ounces mushrooms, sliced
2 slices bacon, cut into
   1-inch pieces
1 tablespoon tomato paste
2 cups dry red wine
1/4 cup (1/2 stick) butter
1/4 cup all-purpose flour
4 to 6 cups beef broth
Salt and freshly ground
   pepper to taste
Enriched beef bouillon base
   (optional)

RED WINE VEGETABLE SAUCE: Melt 1/4 cup butter in a wide 3-quart saucepan. Add the carrots, celery, leeks, onions, mushrooms and bacon and sauté over medium-high heat for 30 minutes or until the vegetables are dark brown. Add the tomato paste and wine and cook until the liquid is reduced to a syrup consistency. Add 1/4 cup butter and cook until melted. Stir in the flour and cook until incorporated. Add the beef broth and cook over medium-high heat until thickened, stirring constantly. Season with salt and pepper. Add the beef bouillon base for color and flavor. Purée the mixture in a food processor and strain into a bowl.

2 pork tenderloins
Salt and pepper to taste
1/2 cup all-purpose flour
1/3 cup (or more) olive oil
1/3 to 1/2 cup red wine

PORK: Cut the tenderloins into 1-inch medallions. Pound lightly between two sheets of plastic wrap to flatten. Season with salt and pepper and coat lightly with the flour. Heat the olive oil in a large sauté pan until hot but not smoking. Add the pork and sauté for 2 to 3 minutes or until brown. Turn the pork and sauté lightly on the other side, removing from the pan as it browns to drain on paper towels and adding olive oil if necessary. Add the wine to the sauté pan and stir to scrape up the browned bits from the bottom of the pan. Stir in the red wine vegetable sauce and return the pork to the sauté pan. Simmer until heated through.

1 1/2 pounds uncooked
   fettucini
2 tablespoons olive oil
2 tablespoons butter
1 red bell pepper,
   coarsely chopped
2 to 4 ounces Virginia
   ham, chopped
2 ounces fresh morels
2 garlic cloves, chopped
1 (12-ounce) package frozen
   pearl onions, thawed
1 (12-ounce) package frozen
   peas, thawed
Minced Italian parsley

TO FINISH AND SERVE: Cook the fettucini using the package directions; drain and toss with the olive oil in a bowl. Add some of the sauce from the pork and toss to coat well.

Melt the butter in a sauté pan and add the red bell pepper, ham, morels and garlic. Sauté until the vegetables are tender-crisp. Stir in the pearl onions and peas. Combine with the fettucini and pork in a large bowl; toss to mix well. Spoon onto a large platter and top with Italian parsley.

GRILLED PORK MEDALLIONS WITH NEW WORLD PAN SAUCE

SERVES 8

*The idea for this dish was sparked by a similar recipe
credited to Dean Fearing. I had not been aware that you could use
tortillas to thicken a sauce and love the distinctive flavor
the tortillas impart to this one. The pepitas and roasted vegetables
add extra layers of flavor as well.*

1 pork tenderloin, cut into
   1¹/₂-inch medallions, or
   8 pork chops
Salt and freshly ground pepper
   to taste
2 tablespoons butter
2 tablespoons olive oil

PORK MEDALLIONS: Place the pork medallions between two sheets of plastic wrap and pound until thin. Coat lightly with a mixture of flour seasoned with salt and pepper. Melt the butter with the olive oil in a sauté pan until hot but not smoking. Add the pork and cook until seared on both sides and just cooked through.

¹/₂ cup raw pepitas
¹/₄ cup olive oil
8 plum tomatoes,
   cut into halves
8 garlic cloves
1 onion, cut into halves
3 tablespoons butter
1 pound mushrooms, sliced
6 ancho chiles, cut into halves
   and seeded
1 teaspoon dried oregano
3 corn tortillas
2 or 3 (14-ounce) cans
   chicken broth
Salt and pepper to taste

NEW WORLD PAN SAUCE: Sprinkle the pepitas in a large dry skillet. Toast over medium heat until the pepitas puff and pop. Remove to a bowl.

Coat a grill pan with the olive oil. Heat until very hot. Add the tomatoes, garlic and onion in a single layer and grill over high heat until charred on all sides. Remove to a bowl. Melt the butter in a 3-quart saucepan and add the mushrooms, chiles and oregano. Sauté until the mushrooms are tender. Add to the tomato mixture.

Cut the tortillas into quarters. Combine with the chicken broth in a saucepan. Add the tomato mixture and bring to a boil. Reduce the heat and simmer for 20 minutes or until thickened, adding additional broth if needed for the desired consistency. Purée the mixture in a blender and season with salt and pepper. Return to the saucepan and stir in the toasted pepitas.

Toasted pepitas

TO FINISH AND SERVE: Add the pork chops to the sauce and cook for 10 minutes longer. Sprinkle with toasted pepitas to serve.

NOTE: You can strain the sauce and cook over high heat until reduced to the desired consistency, if desired.

MANCHURIAN PORK CHOPS

*Manchurian Pork Chops are so named because of
the Asian ingredients used for the marinade, which adds a nice
glaze to the pork when it is grilled.*

1 cup hoisin sauce
2 tablespoons tamari
   soy sauce
2 tablespoons sherry vinegar
2 tablespoons rice vinegar
1 teaspoon Tabasco sauce
1 tablespoon sugar
1 scallion, minced
2 teaspoons minced
   ginger
2 teaspoons minced garlic

MANCHURIAN MARINADE: Combine the hoisin sauce, soy sauce, sherry vinegar, rice vinegar and Tabasco sauce in a shallow dish. Add the sugar, scallion, ginger and garlic and mix well.

6 (10-ounce) pork chops
4 to 6 tablespoons olive oil

PORK CHOPS: Ask the butcher to French the pork chops by trimming the excess meat and fat from the ends of the bones, leaving them exposed. Place the pork chops between two sheets of plastic wrap and pound 1 inch thick. Add the pork chops to the marinade, coating well. Marinate in the refrigerator for 3 to 12 hours.

Heat the olive oil in a grill pan until hot but not smoking. Remove the pork chops from the marinade and pat dry, discarding the marinade. Add to the grill pan and grill for 5 minutes on each side.

NOTE: You can use thinner pork chops if preferred and allow two for each serving.

LEMON-BASTED RIB-EYE STEAKS WITH BÉARNAISE SAUCE

SERVES 4 TO 6

*This simple basting sauce is used by my husband, Jeff,
for all types of steak, lamb, chicken, pork chops, and veal chops.
He suggests making enough to be able to give the meat
one final brushing before serving. Although he grills outside, I have
worked out the timing so that the meat can be cooked
inside in a grill pan or skillet.*

1/4 cup sherry vinegar
1/4 cup white wine
2 to 3 tablespoons chopped
   shallots
2 tablespoons chopped fresh
   tarragon, or 3/4 tablespoon
   dried tarragon
1/2 teaspoon salt, or to taste
2 egg yolks
1 cup (2 sticks) butter, melted
   and still hot
Pepper to taste

BÉARNAISE SAUCE: Combine the vinegar, wine, shallots, tarragon and salt in a saucepan and bring to a boil. Cook until the liquid is reduced to 2 tablespoons. Cool to room temperature. Combine with the egg yolks in a food processor. Add the hot butter slowly through the feed tube, processing constantly until thickened. Add the pepper and additional salt if needed. Serve immediately or store in a thermos to keep warm.

1/2 cup (1 stick) butter
Juice of 1 lemon
4 shakes of Worcestershire
   sauce
Tabasco sauce to taste

LEMON BASTING SAUCE: Combine the butter, lemon juice, Worcestershire sauce and Tabasco sauce in a small saucepan. Bring to a boil and cook until the butter melts and the mixture thickens, stirring constantly.

---

4 (1-inch) rib-eye steaks
Seasoned salt and coarsely
   ground pepper to taste

STEAK: Pat the steaks dry and season on both sides with seasoned salt and pepper. Heat a grill pan or skillet until very hot. Brush both sides of the steaks with some of the lemon basting sauce and add to the grill pan. Grill for 3 minutes on each side, turning only once. Use a meat thermometer if needed to determine the degree of doneness. Brush with the remaining lemon basting sauce. Let stand for 10 minutes.

TO SERVE: Place the steaks on serving plates and serve with the béarnaise sauce.

BEEF TENDERLOIN WITH STILTON SAUCE OR CHIPOTLE CHILE SAUCE

SERVES 4 TO 6

How wonderful that we can once again enjoy this very special dish without feeling guilty. Thanks to Dr. Atkins, beef, cream, and cheese are back in vogue after years of being taboo. The most important part of this recipe is the method of cooking a beef tenderloin; the sauces are just added attractions that can be changed to suit the occasion.

1 (3-pound) beef tenderloin
Coarsely ground pepper
   to taste
3 tablespoons butter
3 tablespoons vegetable oil
1/4 cup (1/2 stick) butter,
   softened

BEEF: Pat the beef dry and season with coarsely ground pepper. Heat 3 tablespoons butter with the vegetable oil in a large sauté pan until hot but not smoking. Add the beef and brown well on all sides. Remove to a roasting pan, reserving the drippings in the sauté pan for the Stilton sauce. Cool the beef slightly and spread with 1/4 cup butter. Roast at 400 degrees for 17 minutes. Let stand for 10 minutes.

8 ounces Stilton cheese,
   crumbled
3/4 cup (1 1/2 sticks) butter,
   softened
1 cup white wine
1 cup light cream or
   heavy cream

STILTON SAUCE: Cream the Stilton cheese and butter in a mixing bowl. Add the wine to the reserved drippings in the sauté pan; stir to scrape up the browned bits from the bottom of the pan. Cook until the wine is reduced to 2 tablespoons. Stir in the cheese mixture and cream and simmer for 4 minutes or until thickened, stirring constantly.

3/4 cup vegetable oil
2 ancho chiles, seeded
1 1/2 onions, coarsely chopped
Chopped garlic to taste
24 fresh tomatillos, husked
2 canned chipotle chiles
Salt to taste

CHIPOTLE CHILE SAUCE: Heat the vegetable oil in a sauté pan. Add the ancho chiles and sauté until crisp; remove with a slotted spoon and drain. Add the onions and garlic to the sauté pan and sauté until light brown. Remove with a slotted spoon and drain.

Cook the tomatillos in boiling water in a saucepan for 10 minutes or until no longer bright green; drain. Combine the tomatillos with the chipotle chiles, ancho chiles, onions and garlic in a blender; process until smooth and season with salt.

TO SERVE: Cut the beef into 1/2-inch slices. Arrange the slices overlapping on a platter. Spoon either the Stilton sauce or the chipotle chile sauce over the beef.

BEEF STROGANOFF

SERVES 4

*In 2004, Jeff and I had a Christmas party to celebrate our
friends, who had never been so dear to us as the year Jeff had spent
battling lung cancer. We chose to have a real meal rather than a
Christmas buffet. It was a large enough group that a fork supper was in
order, so I decided to offer a choice of two old and reliable main
courses: Beef Stroganoff and Chicken Curry. Because Beef Stroganoff is
not often served, people enjoyed it with great gusto.
Never give up on an old standby.*

1¹/2 pounds (1-inch)
  round steak
2 tablespoons all-purpose flour
1 teaspoon salt
1 teaspoon pepper
2 tablespoons butter
2 tablespoons (or more)
  vegetable oil
1 small onion, chopped
1 pound mushrooms, sliced
1 or 2 (10-ounce) cans
  beef broth
2 teaspoons prepared mustard
1 teaspoon tomato paste
1 cup sour cream

Freeze the steak partially for ease of slicing. Slice the
steak diagonally into strips as thin as possible. Mix the
flour with the salt and pepper on waxed paper and
add the steak; toss to coat well. Reserve any unused
flour mixture. Melt the butter with the vegetable oil in
a skillet. Add the steak and cook over medium-high
heat until brown on all sides. Remove the steak with a
slotted spoon.

Add additional vegetable oil to the skillet if
necessary. Add the onion and mushrooms and sauté
over medium-high heat until light brown, stirring
and shaking the skillet occasionally. Stir the reserved
flour mixture into the skillet. Stir in the beef broth
and increase the heat to high. Cook until thickened,
stirring constantly. Add the steak strips, mustard and
tomato paste. Reduce the heat and cook, covered, for
45 to 60 minutes or until the steak strips are tender.
Stir a small amount of the sauce from the skillet into
the sour cream in a bowl. Stir the sour cream mixture
into the skillet. Heat to serving temperature.

Cooked noodles
¹/4 cup chopped parsley

TO SERVE: Spoon the noodles onto serving plates and
spoon the beef mixture beside or over the noodles.
Sprinkle with the parsley.

Short Ribs with Horseradish Mayonnaise

Serves 6 to 8

*Everyone needs a good short rib recipe. An incredible number
of major restaurants are now serving short ribs. They take this ordinary
dish and create wonderful innovative dishes. Be sure to try it soon
to see what magic is being worked.*

1/2 cup mayonnaise
2 tablespoons prepared
    horseradish
Salt to taste

HORSERADISH MAYONNAISE: Combine the mayonnaise and horseradish in a small bowl and mix until smooth. Season with salt. Store in the refrigerator.

1/4 cup (or more) olive oil
6 pounds meaty beef
    short ribs
Salt and freshly ground pepper
    to taste
1 large onion, finely chopped
1 medium carrot,
    finely chopped
1 rib celery, finely chopped
1/4 cup all-purpose flour
12 whole garlic cloves
1 tablespoon herbes de
    Provence
2 cups red wine
2 cups beef broth
1 (15-ounce) can diced
    tomatoes
1 bay leaf

SHORT RIBS: Heat the olive oil in a large roasting pan over medium-high heat. Sprinkle the ribs with salt and pepper and add to the roasting pan in batches. Cook each batch for 8 minutes or until brown on all sides, removing the ribs to a platter as they brown. Drain all but 1/4 cup of the pan drippings from the pan, or add additional oil to the pan if necessary to measure 1/4 cup. Add the onion, carrot and celery to the pan. Cook over medium heat for 10 minutes or until the vegetables are tender. Add the flour, garlic and herbes de Provence. Cook for 1 minute or until the flour is incorporated, stirring constantly.

Stir in the wine and beef broth. Bring to a boil over high heat, scraping up the browned bits from the bottom of the pan. Add the undrained tomatoes and the bay leaf. Return the ribs with any accumulated juices to the pan. Bring to a boil. Place in a 325-degree oven and roast for 2 hours or until very tender.

1/4 cup all-purpose flour
Salt and pepper to taste

TO FINISH AND SERVE: Skim 1/4 cup drippings from the top of the liquid in the roasting pan and place in a large sauté pan. Add the flour and cook for 2 to 3 minutes, stirring constantly to incorporate the flour. Remove the ribs to a serving platter. Discard the bay leaf from the remaining cooking juices in the roasting pan and pour the juices into the sauté pan. Cook until thickened, stirring constantly. Season with salt and pepper as needed. Serve the ribs with the gravy and horseradish mayonnaise.

Ida's Roast Beef Hash

Serves 6 to 8

*I spent a lot of time during my early childhood and teenage years in
Nixon, Texas, visiting my maternal grandmother, Ida Holmes.
She was a fantastic cook. Every noon meal was a big event and made to
seem so easy. She never used a recipe, but turned out unbelievable
country food. I watched Ida cook this hash many times, but until
I decided to include it in this book, it was never written down.
This is a great winter dish that I often serve with black-eyed peas and
corn bread. It is definitely a recipe worth preserving.*

Leftover roast beef
1 large onion, cut into
 1/2-inch pieces
2 potatoes, peeled and cut
 into 1/2-inch pieces
4 to 5 tablespoons
 all-purpose flour
4 to 6 cups beef broth
1 tablespoon beef extract
Salt and pepper to tsate

Cut the leftover roast beef into 1/2- to 1-inch cubes,
removing and reserving all excess fat. Measure about
4 cups of chopped beef. Add the fat to a heavy skillet
and cook over medium-high heat to render the drippings;
discard the cooked pieces. Add the onion to the skillet
and sauté for 3 to 4 minutes or just until tender. Add
the potatoes and beef. Sprinkle with the flour and
cook until the flour is corporated, stirring constantly.

Increase the heat to high and add the beef broth all
at once. Bring to a boil and reduce the heat to medium
when the mixture begins to thicken, stirring constantly.
Cook until the potatoes are tender, stirring occasionally
and adding additional broth if needed for the desired
consistency. Season with beef extract, salt and pepper.

To Serve: Serve hot in large bowl or individually.

*Note: The beef used in this dish can be from a cheap cut,
as it will only become more tender as it is reheated. I use
this dish so often for company that I usually save any
leftover rib-eye roast to make it. Plan to buy an extra-
large roast so you will have plenty left over for the hash.*

VEAL CHOPS ITALIAN STYLE

SERVES 4

*The beauty of this dish is that the sauce can be prepared
earlier in the day, the chops sautéed before the guests arrive, and
the dish finished in the oven just before serving.*

1 cup chicken broth
3 garlic cloves
1 sprig fresh rosemary
1 cup heavy cream
Salt and pepper to taste

GARLIC ROSEMARY SAUCE: Combine the chicken broth, garlic and rosemary in a saucepan and simmer over medium-low heat for 7 to 10 minutes or until reduced by one-half. Add the cream and cook until reduced to a sauce-like consistency. Strain and return to the saucepan, discarding the solids. Season lightly with salt and pepper, as the reduced sauce will concentrate the taste of the salt.

4 (3/4- to 1-inch) veal chops
1/2 cup olive oil
2 or 3 garlic cloves, minced
8 fresh rosemary sprigs
Freshly ground pepper to taste
3 tablespoons olive oil

VEAL CHOPS: Rub the veal chops with 1/2 cup olive oil and press minced garlic onto all sides. Place one of the rosemary sprigs on each chop and stack the chops to sandwich the sprigs; wrap in foil. Marinate in the refrigerator for 2 hours or longer.

Brush the garlic from the chops and cut horizontal slits along one long edge of each chop. Insert one of the remaining rosemary sprigs into each slit. Pat the chops dry and season on all sides with pepper. Heat 3 tablespoons olive oil in a grill pan until hot but not smoking. Add the chops and cook for 2 to 3 minutes on each side or until brown. Remove to a roasting pan. Roast at 350 degrees for 10 minutes.

TO SERVE: Place the veal chops on serving plates and remove the rosemary sprigs. Reheat the garlic rosemary sauce and spoon over the chops. Serve immediately.

89

LEMON VEAL PICCATA

SERVES 4 TO 6

Lemon Veal Piccata is an easy dish to prepare. The finished product is uncomplicated, but always well received. If you have guests who oppose the serving of veal, you can substitute chicken or pork for the veal.

6 to 10 veal scallops
1 cup all-purpose flour
Salt and pepper to taste
2 tablespoons butter
2 tablespoons vegetable oil

VEAL: Pound the veal thin on a work surface with a meat mallet. Coat with a mixture of the flour seasoned with salt and pepper. Melt the butter with the vegetable oil in a sauté pan and heat until hot but not smoking. Add the veal and sauté over high heat for 1 minute on each side. Remove the veal to a baking dish and keep warm in a 250-degree oven.

1/3 cup vermouth or other
   white wine
1 teaspoon minced garlic
1/2 cup chicken broth
2 tablespoons fresh lemon juice
2 to 4 tablespoons capers
8 to 10 thin lemon slices
1/2 cup heavy cream (optional)
1/4 to 1/2 cup (1/2 to 1 stick)
   butter, sliced

SAUCE: Add the wine to the sauté pan and stir to scrape up the browned bits. Add the garlic and cook until the garlic is tender and the liquid has nearly evaporated. Add the chicken broth, lemon juice, capers and lemon slices. Add the cream to stabilize the sauce. Cook until the liquid is reduced to 1/4 cup. Remove from the heat or reduce the heat to very low. Add the butter slowly, stirring constantly. Return the veal slices to the sauté pan and reheat briefly in the sauce.

Chopped parsley
Additional lemon slices

TO SERVE: Garnish with chopped parsley and lemon slices and serve immediately.

Lamb Rack with Provençal Crust

Serves 6 to 8

There is a recipe for rack of lamb in my first cookbook, but this one is different in that it is coated with a beautiful green herb crust. Because it is one of my favorite company recipes, I felt it had to be included here.

4 garlic cloves
1 cup parsley sprigs
1 cup minced parsley
1 tablespoon chopped
    fresh thyme
2 tablespoons chopped
    fresh rosemary
1 cup chopped white bread
    (about 4 slices)
1/4 to 1/3 cup olive oil
Dijon mustard to taste
Salt and pepper to taste

PROVENÇAL CRUST: Combine the garlic, parsley sprigs, minced parsley, thyme and rosemary in a food processor and process until chopped. Add the bread and process to semicoarse crumbs. Add the olive oil through the feed tube, processing constantly until moistened. Season with Dijon mustard, salt and pepper.

2 lamb racks, Frenched
Salt and pepper to taste
1/3 cup olive oil
1/2 cup Dijon mustard

LAMB: Cut the saddle of fat from the rack of lamb. Season with salt and pepper. Heat the olive oil in a large skillet until very hot. Add the lamb fat side down and sear for 2 minutes or until brown. Turn to sear on all sides. Remove to a platter and cool. Reserve the skillet with the drippings for the sauce.

Coat the lamb racks with the Dijon mustard and press the Provençal crust mixture over the lamb. Place in a roasting pan and roast at 425 degrees for 25 to 30 minutes. Let stand at room temperature for 10 minutes.

1/3 cup red wine
2 to 3 cups lamb stock or
    beef broth
Sliced mint

SAUCE AU JUS: Drain any excess drippings from the skillet in which the lamb was browned. Add the wine and stir to scrape up any browned bits from the bottom of the skillet. Cook until the wine is reduced to 1/4 cup. Add the lamb stock, and cook until reduced by 1/2. Stir in mint.

TO SERVE: Place the lamb on a serving platter and serve with the sauce au jus.

Navarin of Lamb

*Spring is often cooler than we expect, and Navarin of
Lamb is a great one-dish meal for just such a time. This stew is a hearty
dish that incorporates the bright vegetables that herald spring.*

2 pounds lamb
1/2 cup all-purpose flour
Salt and pepper to taste
1/3 to 1/2 cup olive oil
1/3 cup port
2 tablespoons butter
1 large onion, cut into
   1-inch pieces
3 or 4 garlic cloves, crushed
2 tablespoons all-purpose flour
2 potatoes, peeled and cut into
   1-inch pieces
4 cups beef broth
1 teaspoon dried rosemary
2 bay leaves
2 cups baby carrots
1 cup frozen baby peas
Beef extract (optional)

LAMB: Cut the lamb into 1-inch cubes. Coat with a mixture of 1/2 cup flour seasoned with salt and pepper. Heat the olive oil in a heavy skillet until hot but not smoking. Add the lamb and cook until brown on all sides. Remove the lamb to a platter and drain the excess oil. Add the wine to the skillet, stirring to scrape up the browned bits from the bottom. Add the butter and heat until melted. Add the onion and garlic and sauté until translucent. Sprinkle 2 tablespoons flour into the skillet and cook for several minutes, stirring to incorporate the flour completely.

Add the potatoes, beef broth, rosemary and bay leaves. Season with salt and pepper. Bring to a boil and reduce the heat. Simmer for 15 minutes, stirring frequently. Add the carrots and simmer for 10 minutes or until the carrots are tender. Stir in the peas just before serving. Adjust the seasonings and add beef extract to taste.

TO SERVE: Discard the bay leaves and spoon the stew onto plates or into bowls. Serve hot with a salad and French bread.

SPICE-SEARED VENISON TENDERLOIN

SERVES 4

If you live in a state where hunting is a possibility, I would
suggest using fresh venison backstrap in this recipe. In central Texas,
where the deer are not large, the backstrap is quite small.
These are a perfect size for a grill pan, which is a great alternative to
cooking venison on an outdoor grill. I have used the same recipe
with a small pork tenderloin, which is also delicious.

1 venison backstrap
1 teaspoon ground coriander
1 teaspoon ground allspice
1/2 teaspoon coarse salt
2 teaspoons cracked pepper
1/4 cup olive oil

VENISON: Trim the venison and pat dry. Combine the coriander, allspice, salt and cracked pepper in a small bowl and press over the venison. Heat the olive oil in a grill pan until very hot but not smoking. Add the venison and sear for 4 minutes or until brown on the outside but rare in the center. Remove to a platter and reserve the drippings in the grill pan for the sauce.

1/3 cup brandy
2 cups beef broth
1 teaspoon cornstarch
   (optional)
1 teaspoon water (optional)
Salt and pepper to taste
1 teaspoon beef extract
   (optional)

BRANDY SAUCE AU JUS: Pour the brandy into the reserved drippings in the grill pan, stirring to scrape up the browned bits from the bottom of the pan. Add the beef broth and cook over high heat until reduced to 1 cup. Blend the cornstarch with the water in a cup. Add to the pan and cook until thickened, stirring constantly. Season with salt and pepper. Serve with the venison.

TO SERVE: Slice venison into 1-inch slices. Serve alone or with Brandy Sauce au Jus.

Poultry and Other Birds

Grilled Molasses Duck Breast (recipe on page 110)

CHICKEN SALTIMBOCCA AND WHITE WINE SAUCE WITH SPINACH CHIFFONADE

SERVES 6

If I could visit only one place in the world away from home, it would be New York City. I was first served Chicken Saltimbocca in a small restaurant in this amazing city, and I have loved the dish ever since.

2 to 3 tablespoons olive oil
2 green onions, chopped
2 garlic cloves, minced
1/3 cup minced red bell pepper
8 ounces mushrooms, minced
2 or 3 canned tomatoes, chopped
2 cups minced fresh spinach
1 teaspoon dried oregano
Salt and pepper to taste

SPINACH STUFFING: Heat the olive oil in a 3-quart sauté pan. Add the green onions, garlic and red bell pepper. Sauté until tender-crisp. Add the mushrooms and sauté until tender. Add the tomatoes and spinach and season with oregano, salt and pepper. Cook until most of the liquid has evaporated.

6 boneless skinless
    chicken breasts
Fresh spinach leaves
6 slices prosciutto
2 tablespoons butter
2 tablespoons olive oil

CHICKEN: Pound the chicken 1/4 inch thick between two sheets of plastic wrap. Steam fresh spinach leaves just until they begin to wilt. Place the chicken on a work surface and line with the steamed spinach leaves. Spoon the spinach stuffing onto the chicken and press down evenly. Roll the chicken tightly to enclose the stuffing and place a slice of prosciutto around each roll. Secure with wooden picks. Heat the butter with the olive oil in a 5-quart sauté pan. Add the chicken and sauté until the prosciutto is brown. Remove to a baking dish, reserving the drippings in the sauté pan. Bake at 350 degrees for 10 minutes.

1/3 to 1/2 cup white wine
3 tablespoons butter
2 garlic cloves, minced
1/3 cup minced red bell pepper
3 tablespoons all-purpose flour
2 cups chicken broth or
    beef broth
Chicken concentrate (optional)
Salt and pepper to taste
2 to 3 cups thinly sliced spinach

WHITE WINE SAUCE WITH SPINACH CHIFFONADE: Heat the reserved drippings in the sauté pan. Remove from the heat and add the wine. Return to high heat and stir to scrape up the browned bits from the bottom of the pan. Melt the butter in the pan and add the garlic and red bell pepper. Sauté until tender. Stir in the flour and cook for several minutes. Add the broth and cook until thickened, stirring constantly. Add chicken concentrate, salt and pepper. Add the spinach just before serving. Serve with the chicken.

Chicken Saltimbocca

Turkey Hash

Serves 6 to 8

My mother-in-law made this dish a family tradition,
serving it on Sundays at Brady Creek Ranch. It accompanied waffles
as part of a large brunch which also featured scrambled eggs,
bacon, and sausage. Additional waffles were passed with
maple syrup as a dessert.

1 turkey breast
1/4 cup onion, chopped
1 rib celery, chopped
1 bay leaf
1 teaspoon thyme
1 teaspoon salt
1 teaspoon pepper

TURKEY: Combine the turkey breast with enough water to cover in a saucepan. Add the onion, celery, bay leaf, thyme, salt and pepper. Cook for 20 to 30 minutes or until cooked through. Drain and cut the turkey into bite-size pieces, measuring 3 to 4 cups for the hash.

3 tablespoons butter
1/2 cup chopped onion
1/4 cup all-purpose flour
2 cups milk
1 cup light cream
2 egg yolks, beaten (optional)

HASH: Melt the butter in a saucepan. Add the onion and sauté until translucent. Stir in the flour and cook over medium heat until incorporated. Add the milk and cream and increase the heat to high. Cook until thick, stirring constantly. Add a small amount of the hot mixture to the egg yolks and mix well. Add the egg yolks to the sauce and cook until smooth, stirring constantly.

TO FINISH AND SERVE: Stir in the turkey. Cook the hash until heated through. Serve on waffles.

NOTE: At the ranch, the preferred turkey hash was made with wild turkey. If you do not have access to such game, substitute domestic turkey or chicken. Frozen waffles are perfectly acceptable as the accompaniment.

PEPPERED MAPLE TURKEY BREAST

SERVES 6

I taught this recipe as part of a holiday menu class.
Few items have met with more success. The glaze is also good
on veal, pork, or even salmon.

1/2 cup maple syrup
1 tablespoon dark molasses
1/3 cup Dijon mustard

MAPLE SYRUP GLAZE: Combine the maple syrup, molasses and Dijon mustard in a small saucepan and heat over low heat, stirring to blend well.

---

3 tablespoons cracked
    peppercorns
1 tablespoon kosher salt
1 (3- to 4-pound) boneless
    turkey breast
1/2 cup (1 stick) butter,
    cut into 9 slices

TURKEY: Mix the cracked peppercorns and kosher salt in a bowl. Add the turkey and coat well. Place on a rack in a roasting pan. Roast for 15 minutes. Brush generously with the maple syrup glaze and dot with 3 slices of the butter. Roast for 20 minutes longer. Brush with the glaze and dot with three sllices of the remaining butter. Repeat roasting, glazing and dotting once more. Roast for 20 additional minutes, for a total of 1 hour and 15 minutes. Brush with the remaining glaze and turn off the oven. Let the turkey stand in the oven for 15 minutes. Remove to a platter, reserving the pan for the sauce. Slice the turkey and arrange on a platter.

1/3 to 1/2 cup white wine
2 to 3 cups heavy cream
2 tablespoons Dijon mustard
Chopped parsley

MUSTARD CREAM SAUCE: Pour out the drippings from the pan used to cook the turkey. Add the wine, stirring to scrape up any browned bits from the bottom of the pan. Pour into a 3-quart saucepan and stir in the cream. Increase the heat to high and cook until reduced by one-half or until thickened to the desired consistency. Stir in the Dijon mustard and parsley.

TO ASSEMBLE AND SERVE: Slice the turkey and arrange on a platter. Serve with the sauce.

Roast Chicken with Sun-Dried Tomato Vinaigrette

Serves 4

*When I am away from home for a while, my first
home-cooked meal when I return is chicken. Roasting a chicken
creates a beautiful meal, but one that is simple in taste
and is welcome over and over again.*

1 (3-pound) chicken
Salt and pepper to taste
1/2 lemon
2 shallots
2 garlic cloves
1/2 bunch tarragon
2 large sprigs thyme
2 tablespoons olive oil
1/2 teaspoon Italian herbs
1/2 cup water

CHICKEN: Season the chicken cavity generously with salt and pepper. Add the lemon, shallots, garlic, tarragon and thyme to the cavity and secure the legs with kitchen twine. Place in a large roasting pan and rub all over with the olive oil. Sprinkle with the Italian herbs, salt and pepper. Place on the center oven rack and roast at 425 degrees for 30 minutes.

Add the water to the roasting pan and reduce the heat to 375 degrees. Roast for 50 minutes longer, basting occasionally with the pan juices and rotating the chicken for even roasting. Broil for 5 minutes or until the skin is golden brown and crisp, rotating the pan. Remove to a large cutting board.

1/2 cup water or wine
1/2 cup sun-dried tomatoes
   in oil, drained and
   coarsely chopped
1 tablespoon Dijon mustard
1 tablespoon whole
   grain mustard
3 1/2 tablespoons sherry vinegar
1 teaspoon honey
1 tablespoon finely chopped
   fresh tarragon leaves
1/4 cup olive oil
Tabasco sauce to taste
Salt and pepper to taste

SUN-DRIED TOMATO VINAIGRETTE: Place the roasting pan on two burners and add the water. Simmer over medium heat, stirring with a wooden spoon to scrape up the browned bits from the bottom of the pan. Pour into a saucepan and cook for 5 minutes or until reduced to 1/2 cup.

Combine the sun-dried tomatoes, Dijon mustard, whole grain mustard, vinegar, honey and tarragon in a blender. Process until smooth. Whisk in the olive oil and season with Tabasco sauce, salt and pepper. Add to the saucepan and cook until heated through.

TO SERVE: Spoon half the vinaigrette onto a large platter. Cut the chicken into quarters and arrange on the platter. Serve immediately with the remaining vinaigrette.

Coq au Vin Blanc

Serves 6 to 8

Coq au Vin is considered true French country fare. It is a wonderful classic that can be prepared up to three days in advance. It will only continue to get richer in flavor with each passing day.

1½ cups white wine
  or vermouth
½ cup sliced onion
½ cup sliced carrots
½ rib celery, sliced
1 bay leaf
1 sprig parsley
½ teaspoon dried thyme
6 peppercorns
1 (4-pound) roasting chicken

MARINATED CHICKEN: Combine the wine, onion, carrots, celery, bay leaf, parsley, thyme and peppercorns in a small saucepan. Bring to a boil and reduce the heat. Simmer for 5 minutes. Place in a bowl and cool to room temperature. Cut the chicken into eight pieces, reserving the back and wing tips for stock. Place in the marinade and marinade in the refrigerator for several hours or longer.

4 ounces salt pork, cut into
  ½-inch pieces
16 to 20 baby onions,
  cut into halves
2 tablespoons olive oil
2 tablespoons butter
12 ounces mushrooms,
  cut into halves
2 shallots, chopped
2 garlic cloves, sliced

VEGETABLES: Combine the salt pork with the onions in a saucepan with enough cold water to cover. Bring to a boil and remove immediately from the heat; drain. Separate the salt pork and onions and dry well. Heat the olive oil with the butter in a deep sauté pan or Dutch oven. Add the salt pork and sauté until brown; remove with a slotted spoon; drain and reserve. Repeat the process with the onions, mushrooms, shallots and garlic. Reserve the drippings in the sauté pan.

Salt and pepper to taste
⅓ cup vegetable oil
1 cup white wine or vermouth
3 tablespoons butter
3 tablespoons all-purpose flour
4 cups chicken broth
Carrots (optional)
1 teaspoon thyme
1 bay leaf
3 tablespoons chopped parsley

COQ AU VIN: Remove the chicken from the marinade and dry well, discarding the marinade. Season with salt and pepper. Heat the vegetable oil with the reserved drippings in the sauté pan. Add the chicken and sauté until brown on all sides. Remove to a platter and drain the excess oil from the pan. Add the wine to the pan, stirring to scrape up the browned bits. Add the butter and heat until melted. Stir in the flour and cook for 1 to 2 minutes. Add the chicken broth all at once and cook until smooth and thick, stirring constantly. Return the chicken to the pan and add carrots, the thyme, bay leaf, salt and pepper. Simmer, covered, for 20 minutes. Add the reserved salt pork and sautéed vegetables. Stir in the parsley. Discard the bay leaf.

SLOW-BROILED CHICKEN AU POIVRE

SERVES 10 TO 12

*I credit Karen Lee, who teaches in New York, with
the idea for this recipe. It is a great example of fusion cooking.*

1 tablespoon French green
   peppercorns in brine
2 garlic cloves
1 tablespoon dark soy sauce
2 tablespoons spicy mustard
1/4 cup chopped shallots
1/4 cup olive oil
1/2 teaspoon freshly
   ground pepper

SPICY MARINADE: Drain the peppercorns. Combine the peppercorns and garlic in a mini-food processor and pulse to mince. Mix with the soy sauce, spicy mustard, shallots, olive oil and pepper in a small bowl.

1 (3- to 4-pound) free-range
   chicken, split, or
   8 to 10 large boneless
   chicken breasts
1/2 cup water

CHICKEN: Combine the chicken and marinade in a sealable plastic bag. Marinate in the refrigerator for 8 hours. Remove the chicken from the marinade and place bone side up on a rack in a shallow roasting pan. Add the water to the pan. Broil as far from the heat source as possible for 30 minutes or until brown. Turn and add additional water if needed to prevent the drippings from burning. Broil for 15 to 20 minutes longer. Remove the chicken to a cutting board, reserving the drippings in the roasting pan. Let the chicken stand for 10 minutes.

1 to 2 cups chicken broth
1/3 cup sherry
1 tablespoon green peppercorns
1 tablespoon sherry blended
   with 2 tablespoons
   cornstarch
Salt and pepper to taste

GREEN PEPPERCORN SAUCE: Pour the reserved roasting drippings into a measuring cup and skim off excess fat. Add up to 2 cups of chicken broth to make enough sauce. Add the sherry to the roasting pan and stir to scrape up the browned bits. Add the reserved drippings and peppercorns. Cook until reduced by half. Whisk the cornstarch mixture into the hot mixture and cook until thick; do not boil. Season with salt and pepper.

TO SERVE: Cut the chicken into breast, thigh and leg portions. Cut the breasts diagonally into three slices and place in the center of a platter. Arrange the remaining pieces around the slices. Drizzle with the green peppercorn sauce.

CHICKEN KIEV

*This classic French recipe is one of the first truly "fancy"
dishes I ever prepared, and it still one of my all-time
favorites. It contains a certain magic, for when properly prepared
and fried, the herbed butter becomes the sauce and makes
a wonderful statement as it flows out onto the plate.*

Chilled unsalted butter
Lemon juice
Chopped chives, or a mixture
  of tarragon and parsley
Salt and pepper to taste

HERBED BUTTER: Combine butter, lemon juice, chives, salt and pepper in a bowl and mix until smooth. Shape into 1-inch balls and place in the freezer for 30 minutes.

4 skinless chicken breasts
  with the small fillets,
  with or without the wing
  bone attached
Salt and pepper to taste
2 eggs
1 tablespoon water
1 cup all-purpose flour
2 cups dry white bread crumbs
Vegetable oil for deep-frying

CHICKEN: Place one chicken breast with its fillet at a time on a sheet of plastic wrap on a work surface. Cover with a second sheet of plastic wrap. Pound 1/8 inch thick with the flat side of a meat cleaver until the pieces are pounded together; overlapping any edges that appear to tear slightly and pound again to join the tear.

Remove the plastic wrap and sprinkle the chicken with salt and pepper. Place one frozen herbed butter ball on each piece of chicken and wrap the chicken to enclose the butter completely. Beat the eggs with the water in a bowl. Coat the chicken rolls with flour, then dip into the egg mixture and coat with the bread crumbs.

Heat vegetable oil to 360 degrees on a deep-frying thermometer or until hot but not smoking. Add the chicken rolls and deep-fry for 5 minutes or until golden brown and the butter begins to come out. Remove to a serving dish to serve immediately or remove to a baking dish to reheat for no more than 10 minutes.

NOTE: If you plan to freeze the chicken rolls after frying, fry them for a shorter time. Drain on paper towels and wrap each separately in heavy foil. Place in the freezer while still hot. To reheat, unwrap and place frozen on a baking sheet. Bake at 400 degrees for 25 minutes or just the butter begins to appear from the center.

CHICKEN FRANCESE WITH LEMON AND PECORINO CHEESE

SERVES 4

*A complaint of my husband is that once I cook something successfully,
I never serve it again. When reviewing recipes for this book,
I revisited this dish, and even I wondered why it was not a staple on our table.
It is a simple chicken dish using a classic beurre blanc as the sauce.*

1 pound boneless skinless
   chicken breasts
Salt and pepper to taste
1 to 1¹/2 cups (4 to 6 ounces)
   finely grated pecorino cheese
¹/3 cup chopped fresh parsley
3 eggs, beaten
Flour seasoned with salt
   and pepper
2 tablespoons butter
¹/2 cup olive oil

CHICKEN: Cut the chicken into serving pieces and pound thin between two sheets of waxed paper. Season the chicken with salt and pepper. Mix the cheese and parsley in a shallow dish. Add the eggs gradually, whisking until well mixed. Dip the chicken into the egg mixture, allowing the excess to drip off. Coat lightly with the seasoned flour. Place on a plate.

Melt the butter with the olive oil in a sauté pan large enough to hold three chicken cutlets in a single layer. Heat over high heat and add the chicken. Cook for about 2 minutes on each side or just until golden brown on the outside and cooked through, turning once. Remove the chicken to a baking sheet and reserve the drippings in the sauté pan.

¹/3 to ¹/2 cup white wine
1 cup chicken broth
6 thin lemon slices
¹/4 to ¹/2 cup (¹/2 to 1 stick)
   butter, sliced

BEURRE BLANC SAUCE: Pour the excess drippings from the reserved sauté pan. Place the pan over high heat and add the wine. Cook until reduced to 2 tablespoons. Add the chicken broth and lemon slices. Boil for 5 minutes. Remove the lemon slices and boil the sauce until reduced to ¹/2 cup. Remove from the heat or reduce the heat to very low. Add the butter 1 tablespoon at a time and cook over low heat until thickened. To hold for later service, reheat the reduced mixture gently and add the butter at serving time.

¹/4 cup chopped Italian parsley
Lemon slices

TO FINISH AND SERVE: Reheat the cutlets at 400 degrees for 10 minutes. Remove to a serving platter or individual plates. Sprinkle with the chopped parsley and garnish with lemon slices. Serve with beurre blanc sauce.

Cilantro-Stuffed Chicken Breast

Serves 4 to 6

*Southwest cuisine is now an integral part of our eating habits. Below is
a good example of the wonderful flavors the cuisine offers.*

---

2 tablespoons vegetable oil
4 garlic cloves, chopped
1 cup chopped onion
1/3 cup chopped cilantro
1/2 teaspoon salt
4 to 6 boneless skinless
   chicken breasts
Salt and freshly ground
   pepper to taste
1/3 cup vegetable oil

CHICKEN: Heat 2 tablespoons vegetable oil in a sauté pan. Add the garlic and onion and sauté until tender. Combine with the cilantro in a mini-food processor and process until minced. Season with 1/2 teaspoon salt. Cut a horizontal pocket in each chicken breast, cutting three-fourths of the way through the center; make an opening about 2 inches wide. Stuff 1 to 2 tablespoons of the cilantro mixture into the pockets and press to close. Season with salt and pepper to taste. Heat a grill pan until very hot and add 1/3 cup vegetable oil. Sauté the chicken in the oil for 2 minutes on each side. Remove to a baking pan.

---

4 to 6 poblano chiles
2 to 3 tablespoons vegetable oil
3 garlic cloves, minced
1 large onion, chopped
3 cups (or more) chicken broth
Salt and pepper to taste
1/2 cup heavy cream (optional)

POBLANO CHILE SAUCE: Broil the chiles on a broiler pan until charred on all sides. Cool and remove the skins; rinse out the seeds. Heat the vegetable oil in a sauté pan. Add the garlic and onion; sauté until tender. Add the chicken broth and chiles and simmer for 15 minutes. Purée in a blender, adding additional chicken broth if needed for the desired consistency. Season with salt and pepper. Combine with the cream in a sauté pan.

---

6 ancho chiles
2 tablespoons vegetable oil
3 Roma tomatoes, cut into
   halves and cored
2 garlic cloves
1/2 onion, cut into 4 pieces
1 tablespoon honey
2 cups chicken broth
2 tablespoons fresh lime juice
Salt to taste

ANCHO CHILE SAUCE: Discard the seeds and stems from the chiles and combine with enough water to cover in a saucepan. Cook for 10 to 15 minutes or until tender; drain. Heat a comal or iron skillet until very hot. Add the vegetable oil. Add the tomatoes, garlic and onion and cook over high heat until charred.

Combine the chiles, charred vegetables, honey, chicken broth and lime juice in a blender and process until smooth. Season with salt and spoon into a saucepan.

TO FINISH AND SERVE: Reheat the chicken and sauces. Spoon the poblano chile sauce onto half of each serving plate and the ancho chile sauce onto the other half. Place the chicken in the center.

Tarragon Chicken Breasts in Pastry with Wild Mushroom Sauce

Serves 4

*I taught this recipe in the early 80s and brought it back in
the late 90s as a main course for a Valentine menu. For that occasion,
I decorated it with hearts and flowers. The pastry is done in a food
processor and is easy and foolproof.*

½ cup (1 stick) butter,
  chopped
4 ounces cream
  cheese, chopped
1 cup all-purpose flour

PASTRY: Combine the butter and cream cheese in a food processor fitted with a steel blade and process until smooth. Add the flour and process until the mixture leaves the side of the bowl. Shape into a ball and wrap with plastic wrap. Chill in the refrigerator for 30 minutes.

4 boneless skinless
  chicken breasts
Salt and pepper to taste
2 tablespoons butter
1 large leek, thinly sliced
8 ounces shiitake
  mushrooms, sliced
1 tablespoon chopped fresh
  tarragon, or 1 teaspoon
  dried tarragon
Equal parts butter and
  vegetable oil for browning
  the chicken
1 egg
1 tablespoon water

CHICKEN: Pound the chicken thin between two sheets of plastic wrap. Season with salt and pepper. Melt 2 tablespoons butter in a sauté pan and add the leek and mushrooms. Sauté until tender. Stir in the tarragon. Remove from the heat and cool. Place 1 to 2 tablespoons of the mushroom mixture on each chicken breast and fold the chicken in half to enclose the filling. Season with salt and pepper. Sauté in butter and vegetable oil in a sauté pan until brown on both sides. Remove the chicken to a plate and reserve the drippings in the sauté pan.

Roll the pastry on a lightly floured work surface. Cut into four portions and place one chicken breast on each portion; wrap the pastry to enclose the chicken and place on a greased baking sheet. Beat the egg with the water in a cup and brush on the chicken rolls. Cut flowers, hearts or other designs from any remaining pastry scraps and press lightly onto the rolls; brush with the egg mixture. Bake at 400 degrees for 30 minutes or until golden brown.

1 ounce dried morel
  mushrooms
2 tablespoons Cognac
3 tablespoons butter
1 leek, white portion only,
  thinly sliced
8 to 12 ounces fresh
  wild mushrooms
3 tablespoons all-purpose flour
2 tablespoons chopped
  fresh tarragon
2 cups (or more) chicken broth
Chicken extract, salt and
  pepper to taste

WILD MUSHROOM SAUCE: Combine the dried mushrooms with enough water to cover and let stand until reconstituted; drain. Heat the reserved drippings in the pan used to sauté the chicken. Remove from the heat and add the cognac, scraping the browned bits from the bottom of the pan with a spatula. Add the butter and heat until melted. Add the leek, fresh mushrooms and reconstituted mushrooms. Cook for several minutes. Add the flour and cook until incorporated, stirring constantly. Add the tarragon and sauté for 1 minute. Add 2 cups chicken broth all at once and cook until the mixture thickens, stirring constantly and adding additional chicken broth if needed for the desired consistency. Season with chicken extract, salt and pepper.

TO SERVE: Place the chicken pastries on plates and serve with the wild mushroom sauce.

Chicken Curry with "The Boys"

*Curry has become so popular again that I felt the need to include a
classic chicken curry in this book. The addition of apple to the sauce is
a must. Enjoy the boys, or condiments; they make the dish fun.*

1 chicken
1/4 onion, chopped
1/2 rib celery, chopped
1 bay leaf
1 teaspoon dried oregano
1 teaspoon salt
Pepper to taste

CHICKEN: Combine the chicken with the onion, celery, bay leaf, oregano, salt, pepper and enough water to cover in a saucepan. Cook until the chicken is very tender; drain. Chop the chicken into 1/2-inch pieces and measure 4 to 6 cups for the curry.

2 tablespoons butter
1 1/2 cups finely chopped apples
1/2 cup chopped onion
1 garlic clove, minced
2 tablespoons all-purpose flour
2 to 3 tablespoons
   curry powder
1 teaspoon salt
2 cups milk

CURRY: Melt the butter in a saucepan. Add the apples, onion and garlic and sauté for several minutes. Add the flour, curry powder and salt. Cook over low heat for 1 to 2 minutes. Add the milk all at once and increase the heat to medium-high. Cook until thickened, stirring constantly. Add the chicken and mix well.

4 to 6 cups cooked rice
Chutney
Chopped peanuts
Raisins
Chopped crisp-fried bacon
Chopped hard-cooked egg
Chopped green onions
Shredded coconut

TO SERVE WITH "THE BOYS": Serve the curry with rice. Pass dishes of chutney, peanuts, raisins, bacon, egg, green onions and coconut as toppings.

Duck Confit

Serves 4 to 6

*In our health-conscious society, you may be reluctant
to try this recipe, but as my mom, Katie Wood, would say,
"Live a little!" This dish is worth the calories.*

1 shallot, sliced
6 garlic cloves, sliced
3 bay leaves
3 sprigs thyme
1 tablespoon coarse salt
1 teaspoon crushed pepper
4 duck legs with
thighs attached

MARINATED DUCK: Mix the shallot, garlic, bay leaves, thyme, salt and pepper in a bowl. Sprinkle half the mixture in a shallow dish large enough to hold the duck in a single layer. Arrange the duck in the dish and sprinkle with the remaining mixture. Cover tightly and marinate in the refrigerator for 24 to 48 hours.

3 pounds duck fat (7 cups)

DUCK CONFIT: Remove the duck legs from the marinade and place in a deep baking dish. Melt the duck fat in a saucepan over low heat. Pour enough of the fat over the duck legs to cover completely. Bake at 250 to 300 degrees for 3^{1}/$_{2}$ to 4 hours or until the meat is tender enough to fall from the bones, checking to see that the fat is simmering, but not boiling. Remove the duck to a deep dish and strain the fat into the dish. Cool to room temperature. Store, covered, in the refrigerator until serving time.

Remove the duck from the refrigerator and measure 1 cup of the fat from the dish. Heat the fat in a 12-inch ovenproof skillet. Place the duck skin side down in the skillet; the fat should reach one-third of the way up the duck legs. Sauté until the skin is golden brown. Place in a 400-degree oven and roast for 15 minutes or until the skin is crisp and the meat is heated through.

Let stand until cool enough to handle. Remove the meat and skin from the bones, discarding the bones. Cut the meat and crisp skin into large pieces. Serve as a stand-alone dish, as filling for ravioli or in salads or risotto.

NOTE: *You can render your own duck fat by boiling the skin from a whole duck. Cool the mixture, chill it in the refrigerator, and skim the fat from the top to use in recipes. You can also order both the duck legs and the fat from D'Artagnan (1-800-DArtagnan).*

GRILLED MOLASSES DUCK BREAST

SERVES 6

*After combining many recipes, this has become
my version of Grilled Molasses Duck Breast. I think you will
find the preparation simple but fantastic.*

2 garlic cloves, minced
1/4 cup Dijon mustard
1/4 cup soy sauce
1/4 cup dark molasses
1/4 cup teriyaki sauce
Salt and freshly ground pepper
   to taste
3 duck breasts
1/3 cup olive oil

DUCK: Combine the garlic, Dijon mustard, soy sauce, molasses, teriyaki sauce, salt and pepper in a food processor. Process until well mixed.

Combine the duck with the marinade in a covered dish, coating evenly. Marinate, uncovered, in the refrigerator for 8 hours or longer; the skin will dry out somewhat if not covered and will crisp nicely when roasted. Remove the duck from the marinade, reserving the marinade for the sauce. Sprinkle the duck generously with pepper. Make two large diagonal slits in the fatty skin.

Heat the olive oil in a sauté pan. Add the duck breasts skin side down and sear over high heat for 2 minutes or until evenly browned. Remove the duck and reserve the drippings in the pan for the sauce. Rinse the duck with cold water and season again with pepper. Remove to a roasting pan and roast at 400 degrees for 10 minutes.

1/2 cup orange juice
1/4 cup balsamic vinegar
2 cups beef broth
1 tablespoon cornstarch
1 tablespoon cold water
Salt and pepper to taste

CITRUS SAUCE: Add the orange juice and balsamic vinegar to the reserved drippings in the pan. Add the reserved marinade and cook until reduced by one-half, stirring to scrape up any browned bits from the bottom of the pan. Add the beef broth and cook until reduced by one-half. Blend the cornstarch with the cold water in a bowl. Add to the sauce and cook until thickened, stirring constantly. Season with salt and pepper.

Watercress
Fresh figs
Red chile oil

TO SERVE: Cut the duck into thin slices and fan out on a serving plate. Garnish the plate with watercress and fresh figs. Sprinkle red chile oil lightly around the plate. Serve with the citrus sauce.

CINNAMON-SMOKED QUAIL

SERVES 8

In the spring of 2006, I attended a one-day school at Stag's Leap Vineyard in Napa Valley. This is a great transition dish—"fallish" but good for hot weather.

---

8 domestic quail, rinsed and patted dry

QUAIL: Make a small slit on one leg. Pass the other leg through the slit. Place on a baking sheet and chill.

1/2 loaf ciabatta bread
1/3 cup olive oil
8 sage leaves
8 slices pancetta
Salt and ground pepper to taste
8 to 12 cinnamon sticks
1/2 cup olive oil

PANCETTA SAGE CROUTONS: Cut the bread into eight 1-inch cubes. Sauté in 1/3 cup olive oil in a skillet until golden brown. Place one sage leaf on each crouton. Wrap one slice of the pancetta around each crouton to secure the sage. Stuff one pancetta wrapped crouton into the cavity of each quail through the neck opening. Season with salt and pepper. Arrange the cinnamon sticks in a stack in a stove-top smoker. Place the smoker on top of the stove and turn the flame on only under the cinnamon stack. Arrange the quail on the rack in the smoker. When the cinnamon begins to smoke, cover and dry-smoke over low heat for 15 to 20 minutes. Heat 1/2 cup olive oil in a skillet and add the quail. Sauté until golden brown. Remove to a rack in a baking pan. Roast at 400 degrees for 12 to 15 minutes.

---

2 cups dried cherries
2 cups merlot
1/3 cup sugar
1 cinnamon stick
1 rosemary sprig

MERLOT SAUCE: Combine the cherries, wine, sugar, cinnamon stick and rosemary in a saucepan and simmer for 10 minutes or until the cherries are tender. Strain and reserve the cherries. Increase the heat to high and cook for 20 minutes or until thickened. Discard the cinnamon and rosemary.

---

1 1/2 cups kalamata olives, pitted
1/4 cup sherry vinegar
1 cup olive oil

KALAMATA VINAIGRETTE: Process the olives, vinegar and olive oil in a food processor until blended but not emulsified.

Tiny micro greens
Maroma almonds

TO ASSEMBLE AND SERVE: Toss the greens, almonds and reserved cherries in a bowl. Spoon the greens mixture evenly in the center of eight plates and top each with one quail. Sprinkle the merlot sauce decoratively around the plate. Place three dollops of the kalamata vinaigrette around the salad.

Fish and Shellfish

Sea Bass with Asparagus Sauce (recipe on page 122)

Red Snapper with Black-Eyed Pea and Citrus Salsa

Serves 4 to 6

*The best fish is served as simply as possible, and this
is a great example. The citrus salsa and avocados contribute
to a wonderfully fresh and beautiful dish.*

1 tablespoon olive oil
1/3 cup chopped red onion
2 fresh jalapeño chiles, minced
1 (15-ounce) can
   black-eyed peas
1/4 cup chopped cilantro
Salt and pepper to taste
Sections of 1 pink grapefruit
Sections of 2 oranges
1 tablespoon fresh lime juice

BLACK-EYED PEA AND CITRUS SALSA: Heat the olive oil
in a small sauté pan. Add the onion and jalapeño
chiles. Sauté for 1 to 2 minutes or just until tender.
Add the undrained black-eyed peas and cilantro.
Cook for 10 to 15 minutes. Season with salt and
pepper. Cool slightly and add the grapefruit, oranges
and lime juice just before serving; mix gently.

6 to 8 red snapper fillets or
   orange roughy fillets
1 to 2 cups yellow cornmeal
1/2 teaspoon salt
1/2 teaspoon pepper
3 tablespoons butter
3 tablespoons olive oil

RED SNAPPER: Discard any bones from the fillets and
rinse the fish, leaving slightly wet. Coat with a mixture
of the cornmeal, salt and pepper. Heat the butter with
the olive oil in a large sauté pan until hot. Add the
fillets and sauté over high heat for 2 to 3 minutes or
until brown. Turn the fillets over and sauté just until
brown on the remaining side.

2 or 3 avocados, cut into halves
   and sliced into fans
Lemon juice

TO SERVE: Place one fillet on each plate and spoon
the black-eyed pea and citrus salsa across the top.
Fan one-half avocado on the side of each fillet and
sprinkle with lemon juice. To serve a crowd, spoon
the salsa onto a large platter and top with the fish.
Arrange the avocado over the fillets or around the
platter. Add lemon wedges to the platter or serve in
a bowl.

*Red Snapper with Black-Eyed Pea
and Citrus Salsa*

Pan-Seared Tuna Steaks with Cilantro Vinaigrette

Serves 6

It is popular today to serve fish with a vinaigrette rather than a heavier sauce. The vinaigrette can be prepared earlier in the day and kept at room temperature. The tuna is pan-seared at serving time, and the entire dish is ready in minutes, making an impressive dish quite easy.

2 tablespoons apple
    cider vinegar
2 tablespoons minced shallots
1/2 teaspoon salt, or to taste
1 tablespoon honey
3 tablespoons chopped cilantro
1 tablespoon Dijon mustard
1 garlic clove, minced
1 medium jalapeño chile
1/2 cup olive oil
Pepper to taste

CILANTRO VINAIGRETTE: Combine the vinegar, shallots and salt in a small bowl. Add the honey, cilantro, Dijon mustard and garlic and mix well. Char the jalapeño chile on all sides in a small skillet. Place in a bowl of cold water and remove as much of the skin as possible; discard the seeds and membranes. Mince the chile and add to the vinaigrette. Add the olive oil gradually, whisking constantly until emulsified. Season with pepper and adjust the salt if necessary.

6 (6-ounce) tuna steaks,
    1/2 inch thick
Olive oil for coating the tuna
4 garlic cloves, minced
Salt and freshly ground pepper
    to taste
1/4 cup olive oil

TUNA: Pat the tuna dry and coat lightly with olive oil and the garlic; season with salt and pepper. Heat 1/4 cup olive oil in a nonstick skillet until hot but not smoking. Add the tuna and sear for 2 minutes on each side.

Sliced avocado
Watercress or cilantro

TO SERVE: Place the hot tuna on a platter or individual serving plates. Spoon some of the cilantro vinaigrette over the tuna and garnish with avocado slices and watercress. Pass the remaining vinaigrette.

NOTE: I prefer tuna steaks that are not too thick. Tuna should be cooked rare to retain the maximum flavor.

COLD POACHED SALMON WITH SAUCE VERTE

SERVES 4

*Individual chilled salmon fillets are a perfect choice
for a summer luncheon or light supper. The addition of marinated
cucumbers and green mayonnaise makes it true party fare.*

---

2 cucumbers, thinly sliced
1 teaspoon sugar
2 teaspoons white wine vinegar
1 teaspoon kosher salt
Freshly ground pepper to taste

MARINATED CUCUMBERS: Sprinkle the cucumbers with sugar, vinegar, kosher salt and pepper in a bowl. Marinate in the refrigerator for several hours or longer.

---

3 cups mayonnaise
3/4 cup finely chopped mixed
   herbs, such as parsley, basil,
   tarragon, chives, watercress,
   mint, cilantro, marjoram,
   chervil and/or dill
2 tablespoons fresh lemon juice
1/2 teaspoon salt

SAUCE VERTE: Combine the mayonnaise with the herbs in a bowl. Add the lemon juice and salt and mix well. Store in the refrigerator for up to 24 hours.

---

1 (2-pound) salmon
   fillet, skinned
Salt and pepper to taste
1/2 cup dry white wine

SALMON: Slice the salmon fillet lengthwise and slightly on the diagonal into long strips $1^{1}/4$ inches wide. Hold down the thick end of the strips and roll up into pinwheels; secure each with two bamboo skewers or wooden picks. Season with salt and pepper. Combine with the wine and just enough water to cover in a large saucepan; cover with a wet kitchen towel to keep the fish submerged. Bring to a boil and remove from the heat. Let stand for 2 minutes. Remove the towel and let stand until the poaching liquid reaches room temperature for fish that will be perfectly poached. Chill until serving time to firm up the fish.

---

8 lettuce cups
Fresh herb leaves
Fresh chives
1 red bell pepper, seeded
   and chopped

TO SERVE: Place two lettuce cups on each plate; place one salmon pinwheel in one cup and the cucumbers in the other. Top the salmon with a fresh herb leaf and place a bouquet of fresh chives on each plate. Sprinkle with the red bell pepper and serve with the sauce verte.

SALMON ROULADE WITH PARSLEY PESTO STUFFING

SERVES 8 TO 10

I credit Mustard's Grill in Napa Valley as the inspiration for this recipe.
I serve it with tomato beurre blanc, corn ragout, and fresh spinach.

---

12 to 16 garlic cloves
1 bunch parsley, stemmed
3 tablespoons olive oil
Salt and pepper to taste

PARSLEY PESTO STUFFING: Combine the garlic with enough water to cover in a small saucepan. Bring to a boil. Drain and cool under running water; drain again. Mince the parsley in a food processor. Add the olive oil, processing constantly until moistened. Season with salt and pepper.

---

1 (3-pound) salmon fillet,
    butterflied
Salt and pepper to taste
6 to 7 tablespoons olive oil
3 tablespoons butter

SALMON: Cut a piece of foil 10 to 12 inches wide and long enough to go around the salmon when rolled, with a bit extra. Cut a piece of baking parchment the same size and place it on the foil. Brush the baking parchment with olive oil. Place the salmon on the baking parchment. Season with salt and pepper. Pat the parsley pesto stuffing evenly over the surface of the salmon and season again if desired. Roll up lengthwise and moderately tightly to enclose the stuffing. Roll the parchment and foil around the salmon and twist the ends. Chill for 1 hour or longer.

Unwrap the roulade and cut into eight to ten equal slices 1 1/2 to 2 inches thick. Heat the olive oil with the butter in a heavy skillet over high heat. Add the salmon and sear for no more than 2 minutes on each. Remove the salmon to a baking sheet, reserving the drippings in the skillet for the tomato beurre blanc. Bake the salmon at 450 degrees for 3 to 6 minutes or until done to taste.

1/3 cup white wine
1 cup tomato juice from
    canned tomatoes
1/2 cup (1 stick) butter, cut into
    8 tablespoons

TOMATO BEURRE BLANC: Heat the reserved drippings in the reserved skillet. Add the white wine, stirring to scrapd up the browned bits from the bottom of the skillet. Add the tomato juice and cook over medium-high heat until reduced to 1/4 to 1/3 cup. Cool until very warm but not hot. Add the butter 1 tablespoon at a time, mixing to form a thick emulsion. Place two or three salmon slices on each serving plate and drizzle the tomato beurre blanc around the salmon.

SPICE-RUBBED SEARED SALMON

SERVES 4 TO 6

A wok can be used for more than stir-frying vegetables, as this recipe demonstrates. It maintains such a high heat that the fillet can be blackened without burning. This can also be done in a grill pan or cast-iron skillet using only a small amount of oil, as salmon is oily and will produce enough oil for the dish. Two different herb rubs are included for variety, although the options are endless.

---

2 teaspoons minced ginger
2 teaspoons minced cilantro
2 teaspoons minced garlic
1/2 teaspoon salt
1 teaspoon ground pepper

GINGER CILANTRO RUB: Combine the ginger, cilantro, garlic, salt and pepper in a bowl and mix well.

---

1 tablespoon grated orange zest
1 tablespoon minced
fresh rosemary
1 tablespoon fennel seeds
1 teaspoon salt
1/4 teaspoon cayenne pepper
2 tablespoons olive oil or
melted butter

ORANGE ROSEMARY RUB: Combine the orange zest, rosemary, fennel seeds, salt and cayenne pepper in a bowl. Add the olive oil and mix well.

---

1 salmon fillet, no more than
1 inch thick, skinned
3 tablespoons olive oil

SALMON: Pat the salmon dry and cut in half. Coat the salmon pieces with 2 tablespoons of the olive oil and coat the inner side with one of the rubs. Let stand for 30 minutes. Heat the remaining 1 tablespoon olive oil in a wok over high heat for 5 minutes or until very hot. Add the salmon and cook over high heat for 2 minutes, loosening with a spatula after 30 seconds and shaking the wok occasionally during the remaining cooking time to prevent sticking; this will produce a lot of smoke. Turn the salmon over and cook for 2 minutes longer, shaking the wok occasionally.

Remove the salmon to a roasting pan and roast at 450 degrees for 4 to 8 minutes or until done to taste.

Lemon wedges

TO SERVE: Serve immediately or keep warm in a 250-degree oven. Cut into serving portions and serve with lemon wedges.

GRILLED SWORDFISH WITH
SPINACH CREAM SAUCE AND SPINACH FOAM

SERVES 4

*Although swordfish is delicious served with just lemon and
butter, I have always considered spinach to be a great accompaniment
to fish and have dressed up this dish with a spinach sauce.*

1¹/2 pounds (1-inch-thick)
  swordfish
3 tablespoons olive oil
1 tablespoon fresh lemon juice
1 garlic clove, minced
1 tablespoon chopped shallot
1 teaspoon dried oregano
¹/2 teaspoon salt
¹/4 teaspoon ground pepper

SWORDFISH IN SEAFOOD MARINADE: Cut the swordfish
into 3-inch pieces. Combine the olive oil, lemon juice,
garlic, shallot, oregano, salt and pepper in a bowl and
mix well. Add the swordfish and marinate in the
refrigerator for 2 hours or longer.

¹/3 cup olive oil
¹/2 cup chopped shallots
2 garlic cloves, minced
2 tablespoons chopped
  fresh tarragon
1 cup heavy cream
1 cup milk
Salt and ground pepper to taste
10 ounces fresh spinach,
  stemmed
Juice of 1 lemon
¹/2 to 1 cup milk

SPINACH SAUCE AND FOAM: Heat the olive oil in a wide
3-quart sauté pan. Add the shallots, garlic and tarragon.
Sauté for 1 to 2 minutes. Add the cream and 1 cup
milk and season with salt and pepper. Bring to a
boil and cook for 10 to 15 minutes over high heat to
reduce. Add the spinach and cook for 1 to 2 minutes
or until wilted. Remove 1 cup of the mixture to a
small saucepan for the spinach foam. Process the
remaining spinach mixture in a blender until puréed.
Return to the saucepan. Add the lemon juice to the
sauce just before serving and reheat to serve. Combine
the reserved 1 cup spinach sauce with ¹/2 to 1 cup milk
in the saucepan. Heat to serving temperature and process
with an immersion blender until foamy; keep warm.

3 to 4 tablespoons olive oil
Salt and pepper to taste

TO FINISH AND SERVE: Add the olive oil to a grill pan
to coat lightly and heat until hot but not smoking.
Drain the swordfish and season with salt and pepper.
Add to the grill pan and cook over high heat for
3 minutes. Turn over and cook for 2 minutes longer.
Bake in a baking pan at 400 degrees for 5 minutes.
Spoon 2 tablespoons of the spinach sauce onto each
plate and spread into a circle. Place one piece of
swordfish on each plate and top with the spinach foam.

PINE NUT-CRUSTED TILAPIA WITH CHIPOTLE TARTAR SAUCE

SERVES 4

One spring I served tilapia to a dear friend who was visiting from South Africa. He enjoyed it immensely and asked what kind of fish I had used. He could not believe that it was tilapia, which originated in Africa, because South Africans use tilapia to consume garbage and never eat it. He was unaware that it is now aquacultured around the world. I have substituted pine nuts for the pecans called for in the original recipe; they make a nice crust and do not burn as easily as the pecans.

1 canned chipotle
  chile, chopped
1/3 cup chopped cilantro
1 cup mayonnaise
Juice of 1 lemon
1 teaspoon seasoned salt

CHIPOTLE TARTAR SAUCE: Combine the chipotle chile and cilantro in a bowl. Add the mayonnaise, lemon juice and seasoned salt; mix well. Store in the refrigerator until serving time.

1 1/2 cups pine nuts
1 cup white cornmeal or
  yellow cornmeal
2 teaspoons ground cumin
1 teaspoon salt
1 teaspoon pepper
2 eggs
2 tablespoons water
1 1/2 pounds tilapia fillets
Vegetable oil for frying

TILAPIA: Chop the pine nuts in a food processor. Combine with the cornmeal, cumin, salt and pepper in a bowl and mix well. Beat the eggs with the water in a bowl. Cut the tilapia into serving pieces and dip into the egg mixture. Roll in the cornmeal mixture, coating well. Add enough vegetable oil to a heavy skillet to reach a depth of 1 inch. Heat the oil and add the tilapia. Fry until brown and tender, turning once; drain on paper towels. Serve with the chipotle tartar sauce.

NOTE: You can prepare the coating and coat the tilapia in advance; store, covered, in the refrigerator for up to 2 hours before cooking. You can substitute any firm white fish for the tilapia.

Sea Bass with Asparagus Sauce

Serves 4

In 2002, I led a group to Le Manoir outside of London. On the way, we had the pleasure of eating at Gordon Ramsay, one of the best restaurants in London at that time. This recipe is an adaptation of one found in his cookbook. Sea bass, in my opinion, is truly the "caviar" of all fish, and the price seems to support this view.

2 bunches asparagus
2 to 3 tablespoons olive oil
1/3 cup chopped shallots
1 sprig fresh tarragon
2 to 3 (8-ounce) bottles
    clam juice
1 large handful spinach
2 tablespoons heavy cream
    (optional)
Salt and pepper to taste

ASPARAGUS SAUCE: Cut off and discard any woody asparagus stems and cut the remaining spears into 1-inch pieces. Heat the olive oil in a sauté pan. Add the asparagus and shallots. Sauté until the shallots are translucent and the asparagus is bright green. Add the tarragon and enough clam juice to cover the asparagus. Simmer until the asparagus is tender. Add the spinach and cook until wilted. Purée the mixture in a blender, adding additional clam juice if needed for the desired consistency. Add the cream and process until smooth. Season with salt and pepper.

2 pounds sea bass, halibut
    or cod fillets
1 cup all-purpose flour
    seasoned with salt and
    ground pepper to taste
2 tablespoons olive oil
2 tablespoons butter

SEA BASS: Pat the fish dry and cut into serving pieces; coat with the seasoned flour. Heat the olive oil with the butter in a nonstick sauté pan. Add the fish and cook for 2 to 3 minutes on each side or until brown and cooked through.

TO SERVE: Reheat the asparagus sauce and spoon onto serving plates. Place the fish in the sauce.

Sole Amandine

Serves 4 to 6

*As I was selecting recipes for this book, I tested many different
preparations for sole. At the last minute, I decided that it
is best served simply in the classic style, sautéed with lemon and butter.
You will not go wrong using the same method for trout, bass, or any
flaky white fish. Although it must be done at the last minute,
it comes together so quickly and easily that it can be served for company.*

---

8 to 10 Dover sole or
    flounder fillets
1 cup all-purpose flour
    seasoned with salt and
    pepper to taste
3 tablespoons butter
3 tablespoons vegetable oil

SOLE: Pat the sole fillets dry and coat lightly with the seasoned flour. Heat the butter with the vegetable oil in a sauté pan until the butter is bubbly. Add the sole and cook over medium-high heat until brown on both sides, turning once. Remove to a platter, reserving the drippings in the sauté pan.

---

2 lemons, cut into halves
6 tablespoons butter
4 ounces thinly sliced almonds

ALMOND BUTTER SAUCE: Squeeze the juice from the lemons directly into the hot sauté pan. Cook over medium heat, stirring to scrape up the browned bits from the bottom of the pan. Add the butter and almonds. Sauté for 1 minute.

TO SERVE: Place the sole fillets on serving plates and top with the almond butter sauce.

GOUGONETTES OF SOLE OR FLOUNDER

MAKES 36

*When I married Jeff I became acquainted with the Argyle Club
in San Antonio, which was started by Jeff's mother, Betty Moorman,
to benefit biomedical research. This dish was a regularly
featured menu item at the club at that time, served with old-fashioned
fried tater tots. I revived it in 2006 to serve as an appetizer at a
Super Bowl party, just to test its popularity. It met with rave reviews,
which I consider a double success as it was served with such
Super Bowl staples as nachos.*

1/2 cup chopped drained
   dill pickle
1/3 cup finely chopped
   drained capers
1/3 cup chopped onion
1 1/2 cups mayonnaise
Juice of 1/2 lemon
Salt or seasoned salt to taste

CAPER TARTAR SAUCE: Combine the dill pickle, capers
and onion in a bowl. Add the mayonnaise and lemon
juice and mix well. Season with salt. Store in the
refrigerator for up to 24 hours.

---

3 pounds skinless sole or
   flounder fillets
3 eggs
1 cup milk
3 tablespoons vegetable oil
2 to 3 cups all-purpose flour
   seasoned with salt
   and pepper
6 cups fresh white bread crumbs
Vegetable oil for deep-frying

GOUGONETTES: Cut the fish fillets into 3/4×3-inch
fingers for a main course and into 1×2-inch pieces
for appetizers. Beat the eggs with the milk and
3 tablespoons vegetable oil in a bowl. Coat the
fish with the seasoned flour. Dip into the egg mixture
and then into the bread crumbs, coating well.

Add enough vegetable oil to a large skillet to cover
the fish and heat until hot but not smoking. Add the fish
and deep-fry until golden brown. Drain on paper towels.

Parsley sprigs
Lemon slices
Fried parsley

TO SERVE: Mound the fish on a heated platter. Garnish
with parsley sprigs and lemon slices and serve with the
caper tartar sauce and fried parsley.

SAUTÉED SCALLOPS ON PURÉED CARROTS WITH EDAMAME

SERVES 6 TO 8

*I discovered a world of wonderful food on a recent trip to
the Pacific Northwest. The dishes are simply prepared,
but reach spectacular heights by using only the freshest ingredients.
This dish is a perfect example. Use organic carrots and large
sea scallops to create a glamorous, yet simple, company dish.*

4 cups coarsely chopped
  peeled carrots
1 tablespoon salt
1 teaspoon sugar
2 to 3 tablespoons olive oil
1/2 cup chopped onion
2 garlic cloves, minced
1 pinch of saffron threads
3 cups (or more) chicken broth
1/3 cup heavy cream
Salt to taste

PURÉED CARROTS: Combine the carrots, 1 tablespoon salt
and the sugar with enough water to cover in a saucepan.
Bring to a boil and cook for 15 minutes or until tender.
Drain and refresh in cold water; drain again.

Heat the olive oil in a 3-quart saucepan. Add the
onion, garlic and saffron. Sauté over medium heat
until the vegetables are tender. Add the carrots,
chicken broth and cream. Bring to a boil and cook
for 5 minutes or until slightly thickened. Process
in a blender until very smooth, adding additional
chicken broth if needed for the desired consistency.
Season with salt to taste.

12 to 16 large sea scallops
Salt and ground pepper
  to taste
1/3 cup olive oil
1/3 cup butter

SCALLOPS: Pat the scallops dry and season with salt and
pepper. Heat the olive oil and butter in a sauté pan
until hot but not smoking. Add the scallops and sauté
on one side for 2 to 3 minutes or until brown. Turn
the scallops over and sauté for 1 to 2 minutes longer
or until cooked through. Keep warm.

8 ounces frozen shelled
  edamame beans or green
  peas, thawed
1 tablespoon butter
Salt and pepper to taste
1 cup sour cream

TO FINISH AND SERVE: Cook the soybeans in the melted
butter in a saucepan until heated through. Season with
salt and pepper.

Reheat the puréed carrots and spoon 1/3 cup of the
purée onto each serving plate. Place two scallops in the
center of the purée and sprinkle the edamame around
the plates. Dollop each plate with small amounts of
the sour cream.

*NOTE: You can thin the puréed carrots with additional
chicken broth or heavy cream to serve as a soup. The color
is beautiful and only needs the addition of a dollop of cream
in the center and a garnish of microgreens.*

CRISP SOFT-SHELL CRAB WITH BROWNED LEMON BUTTER

SERVES 4

*After much experimenting, I have decided to use a simple
batter for soft-shell crab rather than a tempura batter. I credit
Jean-Georges Vongerichten with this batter, which produces a crisp
crab that can be served traditionally with a lemon butter sauce
or in a more contemporary setting atop an Asian coleslaw.*

1/2 cup sesame seeds
1 to 2 tablespoons
    minced ginger
1 teaspoon dry mustard
1 tablespoon sugar
2 tablespoons fresh
    orange juice
2 tablespoons soy sauce
1/4 cup rice wine vinegar
1 teaspoon salt
3/4 cup olive oil
1/2 head savoy cabbage or
    Chinese cabbage, shredded

SAVOY CABBAGE COLESLAW WITH MUSTARD DRESSING:
Toast the sesame seeds in a dry skillet, watching
carefully to prevent burning. Pulse the ginger in
a mini-food process to further mince. Add the dry
mustard, sugar, orange juice, soy sauce, vinegar
and salt and process to mix well. Add the olive oil
through the feed tube and process until emulsified.
Combine with the cabbage and sesame seeds in a
bowl and mix well.

1/2 cup (1 stick) butter
Juice of 1 lemon

BROWNED LEMON BUTTER: Melt the butter in a skillet over
medium heat and cook just until brown, being careful
not to burn. Add the lemon juice and keep warm.

11/2 cups ice water
1/2 cup ice cubes
1 egg yolk
1 cup all-purpose flour
4 soft-shell crabs, cleaned
All-purpose flour seasoned with
    salt and pepper
Vegetable oil for frying
Salt and pepper to taste

CRAB: Combine the ice water and ice cubes in a bowl.
Add the egg yolk and beat lightly. Add 1 cup flour and
mix gently; the batter will be lumpy. Coat the crabs with
the seasoned flour. Dip into the batter. Heat vegetable
oil in a deep saucepan until hot but not smoking. Add
the crabs and fry on one side for 2 minutes or until
brown. Turn the crabs over and fry for 1 minute longer
or until brown. Drain on paper towels and season with
salt and pepper.

TO SERVE: Serve the crabs warm with the browned lemon
butter or give them an Asian flavor by serving atop the
savoy cabbage coleslaw with mustard dressing.

Mussels "The Thirsty Whale"

Serves 6 to 8

In 2005, my husband and I spent the month of January in New Zealand. We fell in love with the people, the gorgeous scenery, and the food. One of our favorite dishes was the green-lipped mussels served everywhere in this magical country. We liked them best at a restaurant called The Thirsty Whale in Napier. The chef did not really give me the recipe, but he did tell me the ingredients, and I have re-created this treat for you to enjoy in your own home.

1 teaspoon green curry paste
1 large onion, chopped
1/3 cup chopped fresh
    lemon grass
2 or 3 garlic cloves, minced
1 tablespoon toasted coriander
    seeds, crushed
1 tablespoon cumin
    seeds, crushed
1/4 teaspoon red chili flakes
2 liters coconut milk
3/4 cup Kafer lime leaves

LASKA SAUCE: Combine the curry paste, onion, lemon grass, garlic, coriander seeds, cumin seeds and red chile flakes in a bowl and mix well. Add to a nonstick skillet and sauté over low heat until the onion is tender. Add the coconut milk and lime leaves and simmer over low heat for 15 minutes.

3 to 4 pounds green-lipped
    mussels or other mussels
Bread crumbs
2 cups water
1 cup wine
1/2 to 3/4 cup chopped onion
2 ribs celery, chopped
2 bay leaves
Juice and grated zest of
    1 lemon
2 bay leaves
1 tablespoon salt

MUSSELS: Place the mussels in the sink and cover with water. Sprinkle with bread crumbs and let stand for 15 to 20 minutes; the mussels will "eat" the crumbs and exude any grit. Place in a colander and rinse; cut off the beards.

Combine the water, wine, onion, celery, bay leaves, lemon juice, lemon zest and salt in a large stockpot. Add the mussels and cover. Bring to a boil and steam for 5 minutes; drain and discard any unopened mussels.

TO SERVE: Reheat the laska sauce and toss with the mussels in a bowl. Serve immediately with a great bread.

Grilled Shrimp with Black Bean Cakes and Cilantro Beurre Blanc

Serves 4 to 6

Here Southwestern cuisine is fused with a French beurre blanc.

---

20 uncooked large shrimp,
   peeled and deveined
3 tablespoons olive oil
2 garlic cloves, minced
1/2 teaspoon ground cumin
1/2 teaspoon salt
1/4 teaspoon cayenne pepper

MARINATED SHRIMP: Combine the shrimp with the olive oil, garlic, cumin, salt and cayenne pepper in a bowl and mix to coat the shrimp well. Marinate in the refrigerator for 15 to 30 minutes.

---

2 tablespoons olive oil
1/2 onion, chopped
1/2 green bell pepper, chopped
1/2 jalapeño chile, chopped
2 garlic cloves, chopped
2 (15-ounce) cans black beans
1 tablespoon honey
1 tablespoon cider vinegar
Chili powder to taste
1 teaspoon ground cumin
Salt and pepper to taste
Olive oil for frying

BLACK BEAN CAKES: Heat 2 tablespoons olive oil in a skillet and add the onion, green bell pepper, jalapeño chile and garlic. Sauté until the vegetables are tender. Add the drained black beans and stir in the honey, vinegar, chili powder and cumin. Simmer until the liquid has evaporated. Process the mixture in a food processor until smooth. Season with salt and pepper. Return to the skillet and sauté until very thick and dry. Cool to room temperature and shape into 2-inch cakes. Fry in heated olive oil in a skillet until brown; drain on paper towels.

1/4 cup white wine
2 tablespoons fresh orange juice
2 tablespoons minced shallots
1 teaspoon grated orange zest
1 teaspoon ground coriander
1/2 cup (1 stick) butter, sliced
1 tablespoon minced cilantro

CILANTRO BEURRE BLANC: Combine the wine, orange juice, shallots, orange zest and coriander in a saucepan and cook for 5 minutes or until reduced to 1/4 cup. Add the butter 1 tablespoon at a time just before serving, mixing well. Stir in the cilantro. Keep warm.

Chopped cilantro

TO FINISH AND SERVE: Drain the shrimp and grill or broil until done. Refry the black bean cakes in a small amount of olive oil if necessary to heat to serving temperature. Place one cake in the center of each plate and spoon the cilantro beurre blanc on either side of the cakes. Arrange the shrimp around the cakes and sprinkle with chopped cilantro.

Shrimp and Smoky Bacon on Polenta

Serves 6 to 8

*I was served this unusual dish at a cocktail party
when I was visiting friends in South Carolina. South Carolinians
serve it on creamy grits, but I have substituted polenta
to give it an Italian flavor.*

---

2 cups uncooked polenta
1 teaspoon salt
6 cups water

POLENTA: Cook the polenta in the salted water in a saucepan using the package directions. Spoon into a rectangular glass dish and let stand until firm. Cut into squares and arrange on a baking sheet.

---

4 to 6 slices smoked bacon,
    finely chopped
1/2 cup chopped green onions
3 garlic cloves, minced
1 pound uncooked shrimp,
    peeled and cut into halves
1/4 cup all-purpose flour
3 cups half-and-half
1 tablespoon tomato paste
Salt and pepper to taste

SHRIMP: Sauté the bacon in a 3-quart sauté pan until the bacon becomes tender and begins to render drippings. Add the green onions and garlic. Sauté until the vegetables are tender. Add the shrimp and sauté for 3 minutes. Add the flour and cook until completely incorporated, stirring constantly. Add the half-and-half and tomato paste and season with salt and pepper. Increase the heat to high and cook until the mixture thickens, stirring constantly. Adjust the seasonings.

Clam juice (optional)
Chopped chives

TO FINISH AND SERVE: Bake the polenta at 350 degrees until heated through. Heat the shrimp mixture, adding clam juice for the desired consistency. Place one polenta square on each serving plate and top with the shrimp mixture. Garnish with chopped chives.

Vegetables and Side Dishes

Corn Flan with Corn Salsa (recipe on page 140)

POTATO GRATIN WITH WILD MUSHROOMS AND LEEKS

SERVES 6 TO 8

Such traditional classics can be changed in various ways to make them more contemporary. In this version I add leeks and wild mushrooms. For variety, consider replacing the leeks and wild mushrooms with zucchini and red bell pepper.

1/3 cup dried wild mushrooms
2 tablespoons butter
3 cups sliced cleaned leeks
1 tablespoon butter
4 to 5 cups fresh wild
    mushrooms
Salt and pepper to taste
4 large russet potatoes, peeled
    and sliced 1/4 inch thick
Chopped herb of choice
1/4 cup (1/2 stick) butter, sliced
2 to 3 cups heavy cream
1 cup (4 ounces) shredded
    Gruyère cheese

Reconstitute the dried mushrooms by soaking them in enough hot water to cover; drain and chop the mushrooms. Melt 2 tablespoons butter in a sauté pan and add the leeks. Sauté for 1 to 2 minutes. Add 1 tablespoon butter and the fresh mushrooms and sauté until tender. Stir in the reconstituted mushrooms and season with salt and pepper.

Arrange half the potatoes in a buttered 9×12-inch baking dish. Spread the mushroom mixture over the potatoes and sprinkle with the herb, salt and pepper. Arrange the remaining potatoes over the top. Dot with 1/4 cup butter and pour the cream over the layers. Cover with foil and bake at 400 degrees for 45 to 50 minutes. Remove the foil and sprinkle with the cheese. Bake for 25 to 30 minutes longer or until most of the cream has been absorbed and the potatoes are tender. Serve immediately or hold until serving time and reheat at 400 degrees.

NOTE: To clean leeks, split them lengthwise and rinse out the grit usually found in the leaves.

Potato Gratin with Wild Mushrooms and Leeks

WHITE BEANS WITH FRESH HERBS

SERVES 6 TO 8

A variation of this recipe is in my first cookbook. "Dressed up" canned white beans have such a fantastic taste that I felt the need to include them here. Great Northern beans are one of the few vegetables that are just as good canned as fresh.

2 tablespoons olive oil
1 cup chopped onion
2 garlic cloves, minced
3 (15-ounce) cans Great
    Northern white beans
1 cup chicken stock
1/2 cup heavy cream
1 tablespoon chopped
    fresh thyme
1 tablespoon chopped
    fresh oregano
1 tablespoon chopped fresh basil
Salt and pepper to taste
2 tablespoons butter
1/2 red bell pepper, chopped

Heat the olive oil in a 3-quart saucepan. Add the onion and garlic and sauté over medium heat until the onion is tender. Add the beans, chicken stock, cream, thyme, oregano and basil. Season with salt and pepper. Cook until heated through. Melt the butter in a small sauté pan and add the red bell pepper. Sauté until the pepper is tender. Add to the beans and heat to serving temperature. Serve immediately or reheat to serve.

VARIATION: You can substitute dried herbs for the fresh herbs and just use less. Or you can omit the herbs completely and add pancetta sautéed in a small amount of olive oil. Add spinach and cook with the beans until wilted and season with 1 to 2 tablespoons balsamic vinegar.

NOTE: The eternal question is whether to drain and rinse the beans or leave them in the can liquid. You may choose to do either. I have found, however, that including the can liquid results in a thicker vegetable dish.

BLACK-EYED PEA SUCCOTASH

SERVES 6 TO 8

*The key to succotash is the addition of lima beans. This recipe is
traditional in that way, but we have given it a Southwestern
flavor here with the addition of black-eyed peas and poblano chiles.
Black-eyed peas are one of my favorite foods, and luckily,
canned peas work really well in this recipe.*

2 cups drained canned black-
    eyed peas
2 cups frozen lima beans,
    thawed
3 cups chicken stock
Salt and pepper to taste
2 tablespoons olive oil
1 onion, chopped
1/2 red bell pepper, chopped
1 poblano chile, seeded and
    chopped, or 1 mild green
    banana pepper
3 cups fresh or frozen corn
1/4 cup chopped basil or
    cilantro

SUCCOTASH: Combine the black-eyed peas, lima beans and chicken stock in a large saucepan and season with salt and pepper. Bring to a simmer and simmer for 45 minutes. Heat the olive oil in a medium skillet. Add the onion, garlic, red bell pepper and poblano chile. Sauté over medium heat for 8 minutes or until the vegetables are tender. Add to the beans. Add 1 cup of the corn to the beans and mix well.

Process the remaining 2 cups corn in a blender until smooth, adding a ladle of the bean cooking liquid if needed for the desired consistency. Add the puréed corn to the beans and mix well. Simmer for 15 minutes or until thickened. Stir in the basil and adjust the seasonings.

1/2 cup vegetable oil
2 garlic cloves, minced
1 tablespoon paprika

PAPRIKA OIL: Heat the vegetable oil in a small skillet and add the garlic. Sauté over medium heat until golden brown. Remove from the heat and stir in the paprika. Strain the mixture into a small serving pitcher.

TO SERVE: Spoon the succotash into a large serving bowl. Drizzle with the paprika oil.

VARIATION: You can substitute drained and well rinsed black beans for the black-eyed peas or add sautéed zucchini to the dish. You can also substitute a commercial red pepper oil for the paprika oil.

IRENE'S MEXICAN PINTOS

SERVES 6 TO 8

*Irene Segura has been in my life since I was fourteen
years old. I have watched her prepare this fabulous Mexican dish more
times than I can count. This cookbook inspired me to ask her to
put the recipe in writing. I am grateful, as you will be.*

2 cups dried pinto beans
8 cups water
5 slices bacon, cut into
　¹/₂-inch pieces
1 onion, chopped
2 whole garlic cloves
¹/₂ cup chopped cilantro
1 jalapeño chile,
　cut into strips
1 to 2 tablespoons salt

Wash the beans in cold water and discard any small
pebbles; drain. Combine the beans with the water in
a stockpot or bean pot. Add the bacon, onion, garlic,
cilantro, jalapeño chile and salt. Bring to a boil and
reduce the heat. Simmer, partially covered, for 2 hours
or until the beans are tender, watching carefully and
adding water as needed to keep the beans covered at
all times. Adjust the seasoning, using enough salt to
bring out the flavor. Serve immediately or reheat to serve.

NOTE: *Irene says that it is not necessary to soak the beans
overnight as some recipes suggest.*

SHREDDED BRUSSELS SPROUTS WITH MAPLE PECANS

SERVES 6 TO 8

*This tiny vegetable is either adored or shunned. In seeking
to increase its popularity, I find that shredding the sprouts makes them
seem like an entirely new vegetable. The tangy vinegar and
sweet maple pecans make a perfect blend.*

³/₄ cup coarsely chopped pecans
1 tablespoon butter
2 tablespoons pure maple syrup
1 teaspoon salt
2 pounds Brussels sprouts,
　thinly sliced
¹/₄ cup (¹/₂ stick) butter
Salt and pepper to taste
2 tablespoons cider vinegar

Sprinkle the pecans in a shallow baking pan. Toast at
350 degrees for 10 minutes or until they are fragrant.
Place 1 tablespoon butter in a microwave-safe bowl
and microwave until melted. Stir in the maple syrup
and 1 teaspoon salt. Add the hot pecans and mix well.

Toss the Brussels sprouts in a bowl to separate into
shreds. Melt ¹/₄ cup butter in a sauté pan and add the
sprouts; season with salt and pepper to taste. Sauté for
3 to 5 minutes or just until the sprouts are wilted but
still tender-crisp and green. Add the vinegar and pecans
with any remaining maple syrup. Serve immediately.

CARROT FLAN WITH THYME CRUMB TOPPING

SERVES 6

You will find this vegetable dish both pretty and easy to do every time. It will add a beautiful color to your plate. The thyme crumb topping makes the dish, so don't omit it.

Grated Parmesan cheese
    to coat the molds
4 to 6 cups water
5 large garlic cloves, cut
    into halves
1 teaspoon sugar
1¼ pounds carrots, cut into
    1-inch pieces
1 cup heavy cream
1 cup milk
4 large eggs, beaten
2 tablespoons grated
    Parmesan cheese
1 teaspoon salt
¼ teaspoon pepper

CARROT FLAN: Sprinkle six buttered ½-cup individual molds lightly with Parmesan cheese. Combine the water with the garlic and sugar in a saucepan. Add the carrots and bring to a boil. Reduce the heat and simmer for 15 to 20 minutes or until the carrots are tender; drain. Process the carrot mixture in a food processor until smooth. Add the cream and milk and process to blend well. Add the eggs, 2 tablespoons Parmesan cheese, the salt and pepper and mix well.

Spoon the carrot mixture into the prepared molds and place in a shallow roasting pan. Add enough hot water to reach 1 inch up the sides of the molds. Bake at 350 degrees for 40 minutes or until set.

2 to 3 tablespoons
    unsalted butter
1 teaspoon chopped
    fresh thyme
⅓ cup fresh coarse
    bread crumbs

THYME CRUMB TOPPING: Melt the butter in a sauté pan. Add the thyme and mix well. Pour over the bread crumbs in a baking pan and toss to coat evenly. Bake at 250 degrees until crisp.

TO SERVE: Cool the carrot flans for 5 minutes or hold until serving time and reheat at 350 degrees for 10 to 15 minutes. Loosen from the molds with a knife and unmold onto individual plates or a serving platter. Sprinkle with the thyme crumb topping. Serve warm.

CARROT FRITTERS WITH CHIVES

MAKES 12 TO 25

*I am always looking for good recipes that bring color to a menu.
Once fried, these fritters have a beautiful orange hue with specks of
bright green. They make a great addition to any plate.*

1/2 cup all-purpose flour
1 teaspoon baking powder
2 teaspoons chopped chives
1 teaspoon minced fresh
  parsley
1/2 teaspoon minced fresh
  thyme
1/2 teaspoon salt
3/4 cup water
1 1/2 cups shredded carrots
Vegetable oil for deep-frying

Mix the flour, baking powder, chives, parsley, thyme and salt in a bowl. Add the water in a stream, whisking constantly until smooth. Add the carrots and mix well.

Heat vegetable oil in a deep sauté pan until hot but not smoking. Drop the carrot mixture by teaspoonfuls into the oil and deep-fry for 2 to 3 minutes or until golden brown on all sides. Keep warm in a 250-degree oven for a short while until serving time. You can also reheat the fritters at 350 degrees if fried earlier in the day, but do not prepare them a day in advance.

CAULIFLOWER PURÉE

SERVES 4 TO 6

*A cousin from Atlanta introduced me to this delicious dish. She perfected
it as she prepared it often on the Atkins diet as her low-fat substitute
for potatoes. I think it is a great vegetable dish, and a particularly good
accompaniment for fish. Jeff and I enjoy it almost weekly. The
addition of milk to the cooking water keeps the cauliflower white.*

1 head cauliflower
6 cups water
3 cups milk
2 tablespoons salt
1 to 2 cups vegetable broth
Salt and white pepper to taste
2 tablespoons butter (optional)
1/4 cup (1/2 stick) butter
Light or heavy cream

CAULIFLOWER: Cut the cauliflower into small flowerets. Combine with the water, milk and salt in a large saucepan. Cook until the cauliflower is very tender; drain. Process in batches in a food processor, adding vegetable broth if needed for a smooth but not thin purée. Season with salt and white pepper. Stir in 2 tablespoons butter.

TO SERVE: Serve immediately or process with 1/4 cup butter and a small amount of cream and reheat on the stovetop or in a 350-degree oven.

Puffed Ancho Chiles with Guacamole

Serves 8 to 10

I like to teach this dish because ancho chiles are so familiar in Southwestern cooking and are so often served in Mexican restaurants in San Antonio. When you buy ancho chiles, be sure that they are freshly dried and still soft to the touch.

---

8 to 10 soft dried ancho chiles
2 to 3 cups canola oil
1/2 onion, chopped
1/2 (16-ounce) package dark
   brown sugar
1 1/2 cups fresh orange juice
1 cup white vinegar
1/4 cup water
Salt to taste
1 tablespoon peppercorns

CHILES: Slit the ancho chiles carefully down one side, leaving the chiles intact. Discard all the seeds. Heat the canola oil in a skillet until hot but not smoking. Add the chiles and fry for 1 minute or until they puff. Remove the chiles and drain on paper towels. Discard all but 1 to 2 tablespoons of the oil in the skillet.

Sauté the onion in the reserved oil in the skillet. Add the brown sugar, orange juice, vinegar, water, salt and peppercorns to the skillet. Bring to a boil and reduce the heat. Simmer for 30 minutes. Pour over the chiles in a bowl. Marinate in the refrigerator for 3 hours to 12 hours.

---

3 large avocados
2 Roma tomatoes
1 small onion
1/3 cup minced cilantro
1/4 cup lime juice
Salt to taste

GUACAMOLE: Chop the avocados, tomatoes and onion. Combine with the cilantro, lime juice and salt in a bowl; mix well and adjust the seasoning. Chill in the refrigerator.

Chopped cilantro

TO ASSEMBLE AND SERVE: Drain the chiles and spoon the guacamole into the chiles. Arrange on a platter and garnish with cilantro. Serve cold.

Corn Flan with Mushroom and Corn Salsa

Serves 5 or 6

Corn flan is an extremely versatile vegetable that can be served as a side dish with meats, as a first course, or as a glamorous addition to soup. Place the flan in the center of soup bowls and surround it with a smooth puréed soup of mushrooms, red bell peppers, or asparagus.

3 tablespoons butter
1/3 cup chopped onion
Kernels from 2 ears of corn
1 1/2 cups heavy cream
Salt and pepper to taste
1 egg
1 egg yolk

CORN FLAN: Melt the butter in a 3-quart sauté pan. Add the onion and sauté for 2 to 3 minutes. Add the corn and sauté for 1 to 2 minutes. Stir in the cream and cook for 5 minutes. Cool to room temperature and season with salt and pepper. Process in a blender until smooth. Add the egg and egg yolk and mix well. Spoon into five or six greased 6-ounce ramekins. Place in a baking pan and add 1 inch hot water. Bake at 350 degrees for 40 minutes or until the centers are set and the tops are light brown.

1/4 cup (1/2 stick) butter
2 ounces button
  mushrooms, sliced
2 ounces portobello
  mushrooms, chopped
Kernels from 2 ears of corn
1 tablespoon chopped chives
Salt and pepper to taste

MUSHROOM AND CORN SALSA: Melt the butter in a sauté pan. Add the mushrooms and sauté until tender. Add the corn and sauté until brown. Stir in the chives and season with salt and pepper.

TO SERVE: Cool the flan in the ramekins for 5 minutes or hold until serving time and reheat at 400 degrees for 10 to 15 minutes. Loosen from the ramekins with a knife and unmold onto individual plates or a serving platter. Top with the hot mushroom and corn salsa.

DOUBLE CORN PUDDING WITH LEEKS

SERVES 10

*The unexpected twist in this recipe is the addition of tortillas
as a base. The casserole is best prepared up to two days before baking.
To serve this for a brunch or light lunch, just add ham.*

3 tablespoons butter
4 large leeks, white and tender
   green portions sliced
   thinly crosswise
Salt and pepper to taste
6 (6-inch) tortillas
5 large eggs
2 large egg yolks
1 1/2 cups heavy cream
1 1/2 cups milk
4 cups frozen corn
   kernels, thawed
2 teaspoons salt
1/4 teaspoon pepper

Melt the butter in a large skillet. Add the leeks and sauté over medium-low heat for 10 minutes or until tender but not brown, stirring occasionally. Season with salt and pepper to taste.

Line a buttered 8×10-inch baking dish with the tortillas. Whisk the eggs and egg yolks in a bowl. Whisk in the cream and milk. Stir in the leeks, corn, 2 teaspoons salt and 1/4 teaspoon pepper. Pour into the tortilla-lined baking dish and chill, covered, in the refrigerator for 8 hours or longer. Let the baking dish stand until room temperature.

Place the dish in a large baking pan and add enough hot water to reach halfway up the side of the dish. Bake at 325 degrees for 1 hour or just until set. Let stand for 10 minutes before serving.

CORN RAGOUT

SERVES 6 TO 8

*The addition of mushrooms to fresh corn turns this
ragout into something special. Browning the corn first in a skillet
is a must, as it adds a grilled look to the dish.*

3 tablespoons butter
3 tablespoons olive oil
Kernels from 6 to 8 fresh
   ears of corn
1/3 cup white wine
2 tablespoons olive oil
1 or 2 shallots, minced
1 red bell pepper, chopped
3 ribs celery, chopped
3 cups chopped shiitake
   mushrooms
Salt and pepper to taste

RAGOUT: Melt the butter with 3 tablespoons olive oil in a large skillet. Add the corn and sauté over medium-high heat until brown, stirring occasionally. Remove the corn to a bowl with a slotted spoon and add the wine to the skillet, stirring to scrape up the browned bits from the bottom of the skillet.

Add 2 tablespoons olive oil to the skillet. Add the shallots, red bell pepper and celery and sauté until the vegetables are tender-crisp. Add the mushrooms and sauté until the mushrooms are tender. Stir in the corn and heat to serving temperature. Season with salt and pepper.

2 bunches watercress, stemmed
1/4 cup (1-inch) pieces
   fresh chives

TO FINISH AND SERVE: Stir in the watercress and chives and serve immediately, or reheat to serve, adding the watercress and chives just before serving.

CABBAGE CREPES

SERVES 6 TO 8

*Years ago when I aspired to be a gourmet chef, I
decided to put creamy cabbage into crepes. I have a dear friend who
thinks that truly the best dish I prepare is cabbage crepes.
His disappointment was severe when I did not put this recipe in
my first cookbook. So, Frates, this is for you.*

---

1 medium head cabbage,
   thinly sliced
1 tablespoon kosher salt

CABBAGE: Cook the cabbage in boiling salted water to
cover for 5 minues or until tender; drain.

---

3 tablespoons butter
3 tablespoons flour
2 to 3 cups milk
1 cup grated Swiss cheese
Salt and ground pepper
   to taste

MORNAY SAUCE: Melt the butter in a saucepan. Add the
flour and cook for 1 to 2 minutes or until no traces
of flour remain. Add 2 cups of the milk all at once.
Cook over moderately high heat until the mixture is
thick, stirring frequently. Add enough of the remaining
milk to reach the desired consistency. Stir in the cheese.
Season with salt and pepper to taste.

---

1 cup flour
2 eggs
1 teaspoon salt
2 tablespoons butter, melted
   and cooled
1¼ to 1½ cups milk

CREPES: Process the flour and eggs in a food processor
until smooth. Add the salt and butter. Pour the milk
through the feed tube with the machine running,
scraping down the sides as needed.
    Brush crepe pan with melted butter and set over
medium-high heat. Pour in a thin layer of batter and
tilt the pan until the bottom is covered evenly with
batter. (The less batter used, the more delicate the
crepe.) Cook on one side until the crepe looks almost
dry, like a pancake. Turn over and cook only a few
seconds. Stack the cooked crepes. Repeat until all
the batter is used.

Melted butter and grated
   Swiss cheese

TO ASSEMBLE AND SERVE: Combine the Mornay sauce
with the cooled cabbage. Place 2 tablespoons filling on
each crepe and roll to enclose. Place the filled crepes in
a baking dish. Pour melted butter over the top. Top with
cheese. Bake at 350 degrees until heated through and
the cheese has melted.

NOTE: May also be served with hollandaise sauce.

CRISP EGGPLANT AND POTATO TART

SERVES 6 TO 8

*What a surprise to be presented with a potato tart only to
find that it has a filling of eggplant! It is such fun to create dishes
that have an unexpected taste treat.*

1 eggplant, peeled
1 teaspoon coarse salt
1/3 cup vegetable oil
1/2 cup chopped onion
4 large baking potatoes
2 tablespoons vegetable oil
2 tablespoons (or more) butter
Salt and pepper to taste

TART: Place the eggplant in a colander and sprinkle with the coarse salt; let stand for 20 minutes. Place on a kitchen towel and squeeze to remove all excess moisture. Heat 1/3 cup vegetable oil in a skillet and add the eggplant and onion. Sauté for 5 to 6 minutes or until the eggplant is tender.

Shred the potatoes with a grater or mandoline. Place on a kitchen towel and squeeze to remove excess moisture. Heat 2 tablespoons vegetable oil with 2 tablespoons butter in a 9-inch skillet. Press half the potatoes into the skillet and spread the eggplant over the potatoes, sprinkling each layer with salt and pepper. Top with the remaining potatoes and sprinkle with the salt and pepper. Cook for 10 minutes or until the bottom is brown. Turn the tart over and add additional butter. Cook for 10 to 15 minutes longer or until the potatoes are cooked through.

TO SERVE: Remove to a platter to serve immediately or to a baking sheet to reheat later in a 400-degree oven for 10 to 15 minutes.

Festive Green Beans

Serves 6 to 8

*Green beans are welcome at any meal. This combination
of green beans, walnuts, and raisins makes an especially nice
addition to autumn celebrations.*

2 pounds green beans or
   haricots verts, ends trimmed
Salt to taste
1/4 cup (1/2 stick) butter
2 1/2 teaspoons grated ginger
1 cup walnuts, chopped
1/2 cup golden raisins
1/4 cup fresh lemon juice
Pepper to taste

Cook the beans in boiling salted water in a saucepan for
5 minutes or just until tender-crisp; drain. Refresh in
cold water to stop the cooking process and drain again.

Melt the butter in a large skillet over medium-high
heat. Add the ginger and walnuts. Sauté until the ginger
is tender and the walnuts are browned. Add the raisins
and sauté for 1 minute longer or until the raisins are
plump. Add the green beans and lemon juice and heat
just to serving temperature. Season with salt and
pepper and serve immediately.

Stir-Fry of Asian Vegetables

Serves 4 to 6

*Nothing is more satisfying than a stir-fry of colorful vegetables,
and flat-bottom woks make them easy for the home cook. They can be
placed directly on a burner, making stir-frying a snap.*

2 tablespoons sesame oil
1 tablespoon olive oil
1 red bell pepper, seeded
   and sliced
1 yellow bell pepper, seeded
   and sliced
6 ounces shiitake
   mushrooms, sliced
6 ounces oyster mushrooms
2 cups snap beans
2 to 3 tablespoons soy sauce
Salt and dried red pepper
   flakes to taste

Heat the sesame oil and olive oil in a wok until
hot but not smoking. Add the red and yellow bell
peppers and stir-fry until they begin to become tender.
Add the shiitake mushrooms, oyster mushrooms, snap
beans and soy sauce. Stir-fry until the mushrooms are
tender. Season with salt and red pepper flakes. Serve
immediately or reheat with a small amount of soy
sauce or sesame oil.

Haricots Verts with Pancetta and Pine Nuts

Serves 4 to 6

Haricots verts is a fancy name for tiny French-style green beans. This dish gives these French green beans an Italian twist, proving once again that combining cuisines only adds interest to food preparation.

1 pound haricots verts
1 to 2 tablespoons salt
1/2 cup pine nuts
2 ounces pancetta,
  finely chopped
Olive oil
1 shallot, minced
2 or 3 garlic cloves, minced
1 to 2 tablespoons minced
  fresh rosemary
1/2 cup basil vinegar
1/4 cup (1/2 stick) butter
Salt and pepper to taste

Remove the stem ends from the haricots verts, leaving the other end intact. Add 1 to 2 tablespoons salt to a saucepan of water and bring to a boil. Add the beans and cook for 5 to 8 minutes or until tender-crisp; they will become aromatic when they are tender-crisp. Drain and refresh in ice water; drain again.

Sprinkle the pine nuts on a baking sheet and toast at 250 degrees for 10 minutes or until light brown. Fry the pancetta with a small amount of olive oil in a 3-quart sauté pan until crisp; drain the pancetta, reserving the drippings in the pan. Add the shallot, garlic and rosemary to the sauté pan and sauté over medium-high heat for 1 to 2 minutes or until tender. Add the vinegar and cook over medium-high heat until the liquid is reduced by one-half. Stir in the butter.

Add the beans, pine nuts and pancetta to the sauté pan and season with salt and pepper. Heat to serving temperature over low heat.

CREAMED LEEKS WITH TOMATOES AND BACON

SERVES 6 TO 8

*The wonderful thing about a creamy vegetable
dish is that it can act as the sauce for simply prepared
meats or fish. I feel that you need at least one item
on each plate that is creamy. This is just the recipe for that,
and it can serve as the base for any vegetable gratin.*

6 cups chopped leeks
    (including 1 inch of
    the green portion)
Salt to taste
6 to 8 slices bacon
2 cups chopped tomatoes
2 garlic cloves, minced
2 tablespoons chopped
    fresh tarragon
3 tablespoons all-purpose flour
3 to 4 cups vegetable broth
1½ cups (6 ounces) shredded
    Swiss cheese
Pepper to taste
1 cup (4 ounces) shredded
    Swiss cheese
2 tablespoons butter

Cook the leeks in a saucepan with salted water until
tender-crisp; drain. Fry the bacon in a skillet until crisp;
drain and crumble the bacon, reserving 3 tablespoons
drippings in the skillet. Heat the reserved drippings and
add the tomatoes, garlic and tarragon. Sauté for 1 to
2 minutes. Add the flour and cook for 1 to 2 minutes,
stirring to incorporate the flour completely. Add 2 cups
of the vegetable broth all at once. Increase the heat
to medium-high and cook until thickened, stirring
constantly and adding additional vegetable broth if
needed for the desired consistency. Stir in the leeks and
1½ cups Swiss cheese; season with salt and pepper.

Spoon the mixture into a baking dish. Top with
1 cup Swiss cheese and the crumbled bacon. Dot with
the butter and bake at 400 degrees for 20 to 30 minutes
or until bubbly.

NOTE: *You can also prepare this in advance, store in the
refrigerator, and bake at serving time.*

PLANTATION OKRA

SERVES 8

Okra is a regular part of summer fare for those of us who live in the south. This particular okra recipe has been in our family for years. Jeff's aunt, Jane Slick, was famous in North Carolina for her Sunday vegetarian lunches. This was one of the dishes frequently served along with at least six other vegetable dishes, some fried, of course.

5 slices bacon, cut into
   1-inch pieces
2 cups fresh corn
1 medium onion, chopped
1/2 green bell pepper, chopped
1/2 cup chopped celery
3 to 4 cups sliced okra
1 (15-ounce) can
   stewed tomatoes
1 cup (or more) water
1 teaspoon dried oregano
1 bay leaf
Salt and pepper to taste

Fry the bacon in a large skillet until crisp; drain and crumble the bacon and reserve 2 tablespoons of the drippings in the skillet. Add the corn, onion and bell pepper to the skillet and sauté for 10 minutes or until the onion is translucent and the corn begins to brown. Add the celery and okra and sauté for 1 to 2 minutes. Add the tomatoes, water, oregano and bay leaf. Cook for 10 to 20 minutes or until the okra is tender and the sauce is thick, adding additional water if needed to keep the sauce from becoming too thick before the okra is tender. Season with salt and pepper.

TO SERVE: Discard the bay leaf and spoon the mixture into a serving dish. Top with the bacon.

STIR-FRY OF GREEN VEGETABLES

SERVES 6 TO 8

*I love the idea of an all-green, simply prepared vegetable dish.
The different shapes and slightly different shades of green make this dish
truly beautiful. You can also include green snap beans, green
beans, haricots verts, zucchini, or any green vegetables of your choice.
Don't leave out the chives—they give the dish an added punch.*

2 pounds snow peas
1 to 2 pounds small
   asparagus spears
3 tablespoons butter
3 tablespoons vegetable oil
12 ounces frozen peas, thawed
2 tablespoons chopped
   fresh tarragon
Salt and freshly ground pepper
   to taste
1/2 to 3/4 cup (2-inch pieces)
   chives

Trim the ends from the snow peas. Trim any tough ends from the asparagus spears and peel the large stems; cut the asparagus into 2-inch pieces. Melt the butter with the vegetable oil in a sauté pan or wok and heat until very hot. Add the asparagus and stir-fry until almost tender. Add the snow peas and stir-fry until tender-crisp. Add the thawed frozen peas and tarragon and stir-fry until heated through. Season with salt and pepper. Add the chives just before serving.

PURÉED PEAS WITH GINGER

SERVES 6 TO 8

*When I began teaching in 1977, the only way to purée peas was to use a
food mill or to press them through a fine mesh strainer; it was very labor
intensive. Now thanks to the food processor or immersion blender, this
beautiful dish can be prepared instantly.*

1/4 cup (1/2 stick) butter
3 tablespoons minced ginger
1 (16-ounce) package frozen
   peas, thawed
3/4 cup (or more) heavy cream
Salt and pepper to taste

Melt the butter in a small sauté pan. Add the ginger and sauté over medium heat for 1 to 2 minutes; do not brown. Add the peas and cream. Cook over medium-high heat for 3 to 5 minutes or until the cream thickens slightly. Purée in a food processor fitted with a steel blade or with an immersion blender, adding additional cream if needed for the desired consistency. Season with salt and pepper. Serve immediately or reheat to serve.

HUNAN ROASTED PEPPERS

SERVES 4 TO 6

*This is the Chinese version of Italian roasted peppers.
Roasted Hunan-style peppers are actually pan-roasted by stir-frying
them until they are charred. It is a versatile dish that can be
served as a side dish or added to sandwiches, rice dishes, or a stir-fry
with meat. I prefer to use a wok to roast peppers for this dish,
which will char them beautifully.*

1 to 2 tablespoons light
   soy sauce
2 teaspoons red wine vinegar
Several drops of Tabasco sauce
1/2 teaspoon sugar

HUNAN SEASONING SAUCE: Combine the soy sauce,
vinegar, Tabasco sauce and sugar in a bowl and
mix well.

1 1/2 pounds mixed red, yellow
   and green bell peppers
1 tablespoon salt
1 tablespoon peanut oil

PEPPERS: Cut the bell peppers into triangles and measure
4 cups. Sprinkle with the salt and spread on a tray.
Cover with paper towels and let stand for 1 hour.
Rinse, drain and pat very dry.

   Heat a wok over high heat for 3 minutes or until
smoking. Add the peanut oil and peppers. Pan-roast
by stir-frying for 4 to 5 minutes, pressing down with a
spatula to char evenly; reduce the heat if necessary to
avoid burning. Add the Hunan seasoning sauce and
stir-fry until the liquid has evaporated. Spoon into
a serving dish.

SAUTÉED PEARS

SERVES 6 TO 8

*Pears are a great side dish for duck or game. Select pears when
they are at their peak in the fall and winter months.
The best way to judge their ripeness is to press the neck of the
fruit near the stem. If it is soft, the pear is ready to eat.*

4 Bosc pears
2 tablespoons butter
6 tablespoons sugar
1/4 cup water

Peel the pears with a small paring knife and cut them
into quarters. Cut the quarters lengthwise into thin
slices with the tip of the blade, cutting to but not
through the stem ends and leaving the quarters intact.

Melt the butter in a sauté pan. Add the sugar and
water and mix well. Cook over medium-high heat
until the sugar begins to caramelize, stirring frequently.
Add the pear quarters round side down and sauté for
5 minutes or until tender and glazed. Fan out the
slices with a spatula and serve immediately.

OVEN-ROASTED POTATOES WITH
PARMESAN CHEESE

SERVES 4

*Several years ago I took some classes from Darina Allen at
Ballymaloe in Ireland. After several days of classes, I realized that she
had avoided the entire subject of potatoes. With some prodding,
she gave us her opinion that Yukon Gold potatoes were her favorite
potatoes. Darina believed in simple food, and this recipe is
typical of her style—choose the best and freshest ingredients
and keep the preparation simple.*

3 unpeeled medium
   Yukon Gold potatoes
1/4 cup olive oil
Salt and pepper to taste
1 cup (4 ounces) grated
   Parmesan cheese
1/4 cup chopped parsley

Cut the potatoes into 2-inch wedges. Toss with the
olive oil, salt and pepper in a large bowl. Place in a
roasting pan and roast at 425 degrees for 30 minutes,
turning occasionally. Combine with the Parmesan
cheese and parsley in a bag and shake to coat evenly.
Serve immediately.

FRENCH MASHED POTATOES

SERVES 6

*When I am in France, I am always amazed by the velvety smoothness of
their mashed potatoes. My assistant, Sally, worked hard to duplicate
this texture for her catering. I think she did a wonderful job, and I have
made her recipe a part of my repertoire for special dinners.*

5 large boiling potatoes
Kosher salt to taste
1 to 2 cups heavy cream
4 to 6 tablespoons butter
Salt and white pepper to taste

Peel the potatoes and cut into cubes. Combine the
potatoes with kosher salt and enough water to
cover in a large saucepan. Bring to a boil and cook
for 20 minutes or until tender. Put the hot potatoes
through a food mill. Heat the cream with the butter in
a saucepan until the butter melts. Add half the cream
mixture to the potatoes and beat with a hand mixer
until very smooth, adding additional cream as needed
for the desired consistency. Season with salt and white
pepper. Serve immediately or reheat in a double boiler.

NOTE: *The secrets to success with this recipe are using the
food mill before using the hand mixer and heating the
cream before adding it to the potatoes.*

DOUBLE CHEESE POTATO CASSEROLE

SERVES 4 TO 6

*Although this is a rich dish, it is definitely a good
one for company. The technique is similar to the one used to make a
quiche. Vegetables, ham, or bacon may added to the casserole
make it a heartier one-dish meal.*

3 tablespoons butter, softened
2 or 3 large potatoes, peeled
  and grated
8 ounces cream cheese, softened
1 cup heavy cream
3 eggs, beaten
1 cup (4 ounces) shredded Swiss
  cheese or Gruyère cheese
1 teaspoon salt
1 teaspoon pepper
1/2 to 1 cup (2 to 4 ounces)
  shredded Swiss cheese or
  Gruyère cheese

Spread the butter in a baking dish. Squeeze the potatoes gently and pat dry to remove excess moisture. Place in the baking dish. Process the cream cheese in a food processor until smooth. Add the cream, eggs and 1 cup Swiss cheese; process just until mixed. Pour over the potatoes and season with the salt and pepper; mix well. Top with 1/2 to 1 cup Swiss cheese. Bake at 400 degrees for 45 minutes or until the top is golden brown and crisp. Serve immediately or reheat at 400 degrees for 20 to 25 minutes.

VARIATION: Cut the baked potatoes into individual servings with a 2- to 3-inch round cutter.

POTATO PANCAKES WITH GRUYÈRE CHEESE

SERVES 4

The basis for this recipe was found in Mustard's Grill Napa Valley Cookbook. *If you are ever in that area, you should not miss Mustard's. Instead of making the patties with your hands, I suggest a 2¹/₂-inch round mold with no bottom. Just press the potato mixture into the mold for a quick, neat patty. A student suggested that a tuna can with both the top and bottom removed works just as well.*

2 russet potatoes
1 or 2 scallions, white and
  green portions sliced
¹/₂ cup (2 ounces) shredded
  Gruyère cheese
¹/₄ cup sour cream
1 tablespoon butter
¹/₂ teaspoon salt
¹/₂ teaspoon black pepper
Pinch of cayenne pepper
2 tablespoons olive oil
2 tablespoons butter

Pierce the potatoes all over with a fork. Bake at 375 degrees for 1 hour or until tender. Peel the potatoes and beat at low speed in a mixing bowl until broken up. Add the scallions, Gruyère cheese, sour cream, 1 tablespoon butter, the salt, black pepper and cayenne pepper. Mix at medium speed for 30 seconds or until combined but still slightly lumpy.

Shape the potato mixture into patties about ³/4 to 1 inch thick and 3 inches in diameter or press into a ring mold. Heat a large nonstick sauté pan and add the olive oil and 2 tablespoons butter. Add the patties and sauté for 10 to 15 minutes or until golden brown on both sides. Serve immediately or reheat at 400 degrees for 10 to 15 minutes or until heated through.

NOTE: The real work for these can be done before guests arrive. They can be assembled two days before serving and are even better if sautéed ahead of time and reheated.

SWEET POTATO-STUFFED IDAHO POTATOES

*I must admit that sweet potatoes were not a staple at
my house. As a matter of fact, when Jeff saw me testing this recipe,
he asked if I were trying to sneak something in on him.
Well, I did sneak this recipe in on him, and he loved it. The nutritional
value in sweet potatoes is so high that we should all
sneak them in regularly.*

1 large sweet potato
4 small Idaho potatoes
1/4 cup (1/2 stick) butter
1/3 cup finely chopped onion
1 cup sour cream
1 teaspoon ground allspice
1 teaspoon salt
1 teaspoon pepper
2 tablespoons chopped parsley
Melted butter

Pierce the sweet potato and Idaho potatoes all over with a fork. Place on a baking sheet and bake at 400 degrees for 1 hour or until tender. Cut the potatoes into halves and scoop the potato pulp from the skins into a mixing bowl, reserving the Idaho potato shells.

Melt 1/4 cup butter in a sauté pan. Add the onion and sauté until tender. Add the onion and sour cream to the potatoes and beat until smooth. Season with the allspice, salt and pepper. Mix in the parsley. Spoon lightly into the reserved potato shells and brush with melted butter. Bake at 400 degrees for 25 minutes. Serve immediately or reserve the stuffed potatoes and bake at serving time.

NOTE: To turn these into a colorful addition to a buffet table, use very small Idaho potatoes, just three or four bites to a potato.

ROASTED WINTER VEGETABLES

SERVES 6 TO 8

These vegetables appear as if they were roasted on the grill. They are an easy and healthy taste treat any time of the year.

5 to 7 cups (¼- to ½-inch pieces) winter vegetables, such as beets, carrots, fingerling potatoes, celery root, red onions, parsnips, red potatoes, sweet potatoes, turnips and/or winter squash
⅓ to ½ cup olive oil
2 or 3 garlic cloves, minced
Herbs, such as rosemary, thyme, oregano, sweet basil, dill weed and tarragon

Line baking sheets with baking parchment or foil. Combine the vegetables with the olive oil, garlic and herbs in a large bowl; toss to coat well. Spread on the prepared baking sheets, taking care that the vegetables do not touch or they will steam rather than roast. Roast at 450 degrees for 20 minutes or until brown, turning after 10 minutes if desired. Serve immediately.

VARIATION: Asparagus is also good prepared in this manner, as are baby vegetables, such as tiny zucchini, yellow squash and red and yellow bell peppers cut into large pieces.

NOTE: The foil or baking parchment is necessary for the vegetables to brown.

Pumpkin and Sweet Garlic Timbales

Serves 6 to 8

*I can think of no vegetable that represents fall better than
pumpkin. You will find these timbales subtle in flavor. The garlic,
which is boiled several times to make it milder, is a perfect
addition. If you prefer, you can substitute butternut squash or
sweet potatoes for the pumpkin.*

6 whole garlic cloves
1 (1¹/2-pound) fresh pumpkin
Salt to taste
2 tablespoons butter
³/4 cup heavy cream
2 large eggs
¹/2 teaspoon dried marjoram
Pinch of grated nutmeg
1 teaspoon salt
¹/2 teaspoon pepper

TIMBALES: Combine the garlic with enough cold water to cover in a small saucepan. Bring to a boil over high heat and drain, discarding the water. Repeat the process three times or until the garlic is tender.

Peel and seed the pumpkin and cut into 1-inch cubes. Combine with enough salted cold water to cover in a saucepan. Bring to a boil over high heat and reduce the heat. Simmer for 6 to 8 minutes or until tender.

Melt the butter in a sauté pan. Add the pumpkin and sauté for several minutes until the water evaporates, stirring constantly to avoid scorching. Combine the pumpkin and garlic in a food processor and add the cream. Process until smooth, scraping the side of the bowl as necessary. Add the eggs and process until smooth. Season with the marjoram, nutmeg, salt and pepper. Spoon into eight 3-ounce ramekins and place in a shallow roasting pan; add 1 inch hot water to the pan. Bake at 350 degrees for 35 to 40 minutes or until set around the edges. Let stand for 5 to 10 minutes.

3 tablespoons butter
¹/3 cup chopped scallions
¹/4 cup minced chives

TO FINISH AND SERVE: Melt the butter in a sauté pan and add the scallions. Sauté until tender. Loosen the pumpkin mixture from the ramekins with a knife and remove to serving plates. Top with the scallion mixture. Sprinkle with the chives.

BUTTERNUT SQUASH TARTS WITH PUMPKIN SEED CRUST AND CHEESE LATTICE

SERVES 6

Food preparation is fun when whimsy is a part of the process. Instead of using regular pastry dough to create a lattice topping for this tart, I have used crisscrossed slices of cheese.

1/4 cup roasted salted
   pumpkin seeds
1 cup all-purpose flour
6 tablespoons unsalted butter,
   chilled and chopped
1/4 cup water

PUMPKIN SEED CRUST: Process the pumpkin seeds in a food processor until ground. Add the flour and butter and process to the texture of coarse meal. Add the water and process until the mixture forms a ball. Sprinkle with additional flour and roll 1/8 inch thick on a floured surface. Cut six circles with a floured 2-inch cutter. Press each circle into a fluted metal tartlet pan. Prick the pastries lightly with a fork. Chill for 30 minutes or place in the freezer for 15 minutes. Line the pastry shells with foil and weight with uncooked rice or place a second tart pan on top. Bake at 425 degrees for 15 minutes. Remove the rice and foil and bake for 5 to 7 minutes longer or until golden brown. Cool in the tartlet pans on a wire rack.

1 pound butternut squash
1/4 cup heavy cream
1 to 2 tablespoons butter
1 large egg, lightly beaten
3/4 teaspoon salt
1/4 teaspoon pepper
4 ounces thinly sliced
   Gruyère cheese

TARTS: Peel the squash and cut into 2-inch pieces. Place in a steamer over boiling water and steam for 30 to 40 minutes or until very tender, checking the water level every 15 minutes; drain. Measure 1 cup of the steamed squash and combine with the cream, butter, egg, salt and pepper in a food processor; process until smooth. Spoon the mixture into the cooled tart shells.

Cut the Gruyère cheese into thirty strips 1/8 inch wide. Arrange six strips of cheese on each tart to form a lattice. Bake the tarts at 375 degrees on the center oven rack for 20 to 25 minutes or until the filling is slightly puffed and the cheese is melted. Serve immediately.

VARIATION: It is even easier to make this as a single larger tart or by using a ready-to-bake pastry.

NOTE: You can prepare the tart shells in advance and freeze until needed. You can also bake the tarts in advance and reheat at 350 degrees for 15 minutes to serve.

CREAMED FRESH SPINACH

SERVES 6 TO 8

*In reviewing old classics, I realize that I have taught
creamed spinach over and over, probably because it is such a classic
favorite. I have regularly used frozen spinach and thought
it worked well. This recipe, however, calls for fresh spinach; it definitely
tastes better, and the color is beautiful. Don't give up on
frozen spinach when that is all that time allows, but once you
taste fresh spinach, you may never go back.*

8 cups packed washed
   fresh spinach
Salt to taste
2 tablespoons butter
2 tablespoons sliced shallots
1 garlic clove, sliced
1/3 cup (or more) heavy cream
1/3 cup (or more) chicken broth
Pepper to taste

Blanch the spinach in 1/2 inch of boiling salted water
in a saucepan for 1 to 2 minutes; drain and refresh in
ice water to stop the cooking process. Drain again and
squeeze out as much moisture as possible.

Melt the butter in a large sauté pan. Add the shallots
and garlic and sauté for 2 minutes or until the shallots
are translucent. Add the spinach, cream and chicken
broth. Bring to a simmer and simmer for 2 minutes.
Purée in a food processor or blender, adding cream
or chicken broth if needed for the desired consistency.
Season with salt and pepper. Serve immediately or
chill for up to two days; reheat to serve.

NOTE: *This dish is so flavorful that I truly believe you could
serve it daily without the cream and save the cream for a
special occasion.*

BABY SPINACH AND GARLIC BREAD PUDDING

SERVES 6 TO 8

*Although bread pudding is good at any time, it is traditionally served in
the winter months. This version is a tasty addition to any holiday menu.
I have found that using frozen chopped spinach rather than fresh spinach
is easier and produces the same wonderful result. Just press as much
moisture as possible from the spinach before using it.*

---

3 to 4 tablespoons butter
2 whole garlic cloves
1/2 French baguette, cut into
   1/4-inch cubes (about 3 cups)

GARLIC CROUTONS: Heat the butter in a 3-quart sauté
pan. Add the garlic and bread cubes. Cook over
medium heat for 3 minutes or until the bread cubes
are brown on the bottom. Stir and cook for 2 minutes
longer or until the croutons are crisp and brown all
over. Remove to a plate to cool, discarding the garlic.
Reserve the sauté pan.

1/4 cup water
1 small garlic clove, minced
Salt and pepper to taste
10 ounces fresh baby spinach,
   stemmed
1 tablespoon butter
1/2 cup chopped red bell pepper
2 large eggs
1 cup heavy cream
Pinch of freshly grated nutmeg
1/2 teaspoon salt
1/2 teaspoon pepper

PUDDING: Add the water to the reserved sauté pan.
Add the garlic and season with salt and pepper to taste.
Add the spinach and cook, covered, for 1 to 2 minutes
or until the spinach is wilted. Drain, reserving the
cooking liquid. Chop the spinach.

   Melt the butter in a small saucepan. Add the red
bell pepper and sauté until tender-crisp. Whisk the
eggs with the cream, reserved cooking liquid, nutmeg,
1/2 teaspoon salt and 1/2 teaspoon pepper in a bowl.
Stir in the spinach and red bell pepper. Spoon the
mixture into six to eight buttered individual soufflé
dishes or a buttered 6-cup soufflé dish.

   Sprinkle the garlic croutons on the spinach mixture
and press lightly into the spinach. Place in a large pan
and add enough hot water to the pan to reach halfway
up the sides of the soufflé dishes. Bake immediately at
350 degrees for 35 to 40 minutes or until set, or hold
to bake at serving time.

TO SERVE: Loosen the puddings from the dishes with a
knife and unmold bread side up on serving plates.
Serve immediately or place on a baking sheet and
reheat at 350 degrees for 10 minutes. Serve hot.

Spinach Soufflé Mold with Hollandaise Sauce

Serves 6

*My longtime friend and assistant, Sally Helland,
now has her own catering company. This is a dish she often uses
for her large parties, as it can be prepared in advance
and reheated. She bakes the spinach in a baking pan with 1-inch
sides and then cuts the spinach into rounds. These look lovely
on a plate or arranged on a large platter for a buffet.*

1/4 cup (1/2 stick) butter
3 (8-ounce) packages frozen
   spinach, thawed
5 eggs
1 cup heavy cream
Nutmeg to taste (optional)
Salt and pepper to taste

SPINACH: Brown the butter lightly in a small sauté pan. Squeeze the moisture from the spinach and combine with the browned butter, eggs and cream in a bowl. Season with nutmeg, salt and pepper and mix well. Spoon into buttered individual soufflé dishes or a large buttered springform pan. Bake at 350 degrees for 30 minutes or until set. Cool slightly,

2 egg yolks
Juice of 1/2 lemon
1/2 teaspoon salt
1 cup (2 sticks) butter, melted
   and still hot

HOLLANDAISE SAUCE: Combine the eggs, lemon juice and salt in a food processor. Add the hot butter through the feed tube very gradually, processing constantly until smooth. Keep warm.

TO SERVE: Loosen the individual soufflés from the dishes with a knife and unmold onto serving plates or place the springform pan on a serving plate and remove the side of the pan. Serve immediately with the Hollandaise sauce.

VARIATION: You can also use this recipe as a spinach roll if you bake it in a flat baking pan lined with waxed paper. Use the waxed paper to guide the baked spinach mixture as you roll it up. Unroll and fill with a mushroom filling or any innovative filling you desire; roll it up to contain the filling. Slice and serve with the Hollandaise sauce.

Zucchini Saltimbocca

Serves 6 to 8

Saltimbocca, which translates from the Italian as "jump in the mouth" is traditionally prepared with veal, prosciutto, and sage. This version substitutes zucchini for the veal and is equally delicious. It is an appealing and different way to serve zucchini. It also makes a nice first course served with tomato sauce.

4 to 6 zucchini
1 teaspoon salt
10 to 12 thin slices prosciutto
10 to 12 fresh sage leaves
2 cups all-purpose flour
Salt and pepper to taste
2 eggs
2 cups fresh bread crumbs
1 cup (4 ounces) grated
   Parmesan cheese or
   shredded Gruyère cheese
1/2 cup olive oil

Slice the zucchini lengthwise into thin strips. Sprinkle with 1 teaspoon salt and let stand for 20 minutes. Pat dry with paper towels. Place one slice of prosciutto on half the zucchini slices and top with a sage leaf and the remaining zucchini slices to form "sandwiches." Secure with a wooden pick.

Season the flour with salt and pepper to taste. Beat the eggs in a bowl. Mix the bread crumbs with the Parmesan cheese in a bowl. Coat the zucchini with the seasoned flour, then dip in the eggs and coat with the bread crumb mixture. Heat the olive oil in a sauté pan and add the zucchini. Sauté until brown on both sides, turning once. Season with salt and pepper to taste. Serve immediately or reheat on a baking sheet at 350 degrees for 10 to 15 minutes to serve later.

ZUCCHINI ROLLS AND
TOMATO SAUCE WITH BASIL

MAKES 16

*This recipe serves eight as a first course. I debated
whether to include it as a first course or as
a vegetable; it is adaptable for either. As a first course,
consider adding some chopped ham or prosciutto.*

2 tablespoons olive oil
1/2 cup minced onion
2 garlic cloves, minced
1 (28-ounce) can premium
   tomatoes, chopped
2 tablespoons tomato paste
1 cup slivered fresh basil
1 teaspoon dried oregano
1/2 cup water
Salt and pepper to taste

TOMATO SAUCE WITH BASIL: Heat the olive oil in a
2-quart saucepan. Add the onion and garlic and sauté
for 3 minutes or until tender. Add the tomatoes, basil,
oregano and water; mix well. Cook for 20 to 30 minutes
or until thickened to the desired consistency. Season
with salt and pepper.

3 zucchini
1/4 cup olive oil
Salt and freshly ground pepper
   to taste
1/2 cup fresh basil leaves
15 ounces ricotta cheese
1 cup (4 ounces) freshly grated
   Romano cheese

ZUCCHINI ROLLS: Cut the zucchini lengthwise into slices
1/8 to 1/4 inch wide; discard the outer slices with more
of the peel. Brush the slices with the olive oil and
sprinkle with salt and pepper. Arrange on a baking
sheet and bake at 350 degrees for 20 minutes or
just until tender; cool.

   Mince the basil leaves in a food processor. Add the
ricotta cheese and Romano cheese and process to mix
well. Season with salt and pepper. Place 1 tablespoon
of the basil mixture on each zucchini slice and roll
the zucchini to enclose the filling. Place in a baking
pan and store in the refrigerator until time to bake.
Bake at 350 degrees for 10 to 15 minutes or until
heated through.

Slivered fresh basil

TO SERVE: Place the zucchini rolls on serving plates and
garnish with fresh basil. Serve with the tomato sauce.

Pastas Grains Breads

Corn Bread Terrine with Mushrooms and Corn
(recipe on page 181)

Jeweled Couscous Rings

Serves 6 to 8

*I read a brief description of this recipe somewhere, but
no measurements were given. It sounded so wonderful that I decided
to work with it until it was one I could teach. I originally
taught it as an accompaniment for duck, but it goes equally well
with any fall or winter menu.*

2 (5.5-ounce) packages
   couscous
1/2 cup dried cherries
1/2 cup dried apricots
2 tablespoons (or more) butter
1/2 cup chopped red bell pepper
1 cup frozen tiny peas, thawed
1/4 cup sliced almonds
2 tablespoons chopped
   fresh mint
Salt and pepper

Cook the couscous using the package directions.
Combine the dried cherries and dried apricots with
enough hot water to cover in a bowl and let stand
until plump; drain. Melt the butter in a small sauté
pan and add the red bell pepper. Sauté until the
pepper is tender. Combine with the couscous, cherries,
apricots, peas, almonds and mint in a bowl and mix
well. Season with salt and pepper and add additional
butter if needed. Press the mixture firmly into greased
1 cup soufflé dishes or 1/2-cup round molds with no
bottoms. Cover and chill until serving time.

To Finish and Serve: Bake the couscous at 400 degrees
for 15 minutes or until heated through. Let stand
for 5 minutes. Unmold onto a serving platter or
individual plates.

Jeweled Couscous Rings

Tagliatelle with Cherry Tomato and Basil Sauce

Serves 4 to 6

*Making pasta is quite fun, but a good commercial pasta is
an acceptable alternative. If you make fresh pasta for this recipe,
I suggest that you cook the pasta immediately after it has been cut.
The fresh cherry tomatoes sautéed simply with basil, garlic,
and olive oil impart just the right touch to any pasta.*

Kosher salt to taste
12 ounces uncooked
   tagliatelle or Homemade
   Pasta (page 169)

TAGLIATELLE: Bring a saucepan of water to a boil and add the kosher salt. Add the tagliatelle; cook commercial tagliatelle using the package directions and Homemade Pasta for 2 to 3 minutes; drain and keep warm.

3/4 cup olive oil
12 ounces cherry tomatoes,
   cut into halves
2 garlic cloves, minced
1/2 cup chopped shallots
1/2 cup chopped fresh basil
Salt and pepper to taste
2 tablespoons butter
Grated fresh Parmesan cheese

CHERRY TOMATO AND BASIL SAUCE: Heat the olive oil in a sauté pan and add the cherry tomatoes and garlic. Sauté over medium heat for 5 to 10 minutes or until the tomatoes begin to release their juices and the mixture thickens. Add the shallots and cook for 2 to 3 minutes. Add the basil, salt and pepper. Add the butter at serving time or reheat with the butter to serve later.

Toss the pasta with the cherry tomato and basil sauce. Top with Parmesan cheese and pass additional Parmesan cheese.

Truffle Sauce

Serves 4 to 6

*Truffle Sauce is a good alternative to serve with pasta for a
quick and easy dish. Truffles are expensive, but it doesn't take very many
to impart a wonderful flavor to a dish for a special occasion.*

---

1 cup olive oil
2 garlic cloves, minced
1/2 cup chopped shallots
1/2 cup sliced truffles
1 cup white wine
Salt and freshly ground pepper
   to taste

Heat the olive oil in a sauté pan and add the garlic and shallots. Sauté over medium-high heat until translucent. Add the truffles and sauté for 1 to 2 minutes. Stir in the wine and cook until reduced to the desired consistency. Season with salt and pepper.

Homemade Pasta

Serves 6 to 8

*I am including this recipe from my first book for cooks who want to
offer guests something really special. All pasta recipes in this book can be
completed without going to the trouble of making fresh pasta.*

**2 cups (or more) all-purpose
    flour**
3 eggs

Pasta Dough: Combine the flour and eggs in a food
processor and process until the mixture forms a ball.
Shape into a smooth ball with your hands. Return to the
food processor if the dough is too sticky and process
with an additional 1/4 cup of flour; the dough will break
apart but will come together again. Shape into a ball,
coating with additional flour only if needed. If the dough
sticks while being kneaded, additional flour is needed.

Kneading the Dough: Set the pasta machine on the
largest setting, #1 on most machines; do not change
the setting while kneading the dough. Run the dough
through the machine as many times as needed to reach
the width of the machine; the dough will become wider
each time it is run through the machine. Fold the dough
in half lengthwise when it has reached the width of
the machine and repeat the kneading process until the
dough reaches the width of the machine again. Repeat
this process four or five times. Leave the dough unfolded
the last time it reaches the width of the machine.

Stretching the Dough: Set the pasta machine on
#2 and run the dough through the machine two times;
the dough will be getting longer rather than wider in
the stretching process. Set the pasta machine on #3 and
run the dough through the machine two times. Repeat
the process, increasing the setting to #4 and then to
#5 or until the dough is as thin as desired. Cut the
pasta into the shapes desired.

Cooking the Pasta: Bring a large saucepan of salted
water to a boil and add the pasta. Cook for several
minutes or just until al dente. Remember that fresh
pasta cooks much more quickly than dried pasta.

Saffron Orzo with Pesto

Serves 6

Orzo, which is a Greek pasta, is a good example of the way
that variety in home cooking changed as products from other countries
became readily available here. I did not introduce orzo into my
cooking classes until 1997. The way it is cooked in this recipe gives it a
creamy texture similar to risotto, but it can also be cooked in half the
time and with much less effort. Unlike risotto, it can be prepared in
advance and reheated to serve. Serve it with pesto, as it is here, or alone.

---

1 cup fresh basil leaves
2 garlic cloves
1/3 cup pine nuts
1/3 cup freshly grated
  Parmesan cheese
1/3 cup olive oil
Salt and pepper to taste

PESTO: Combine the basil, garlic, pine nuts and Parmesan cheese in a food processor and process until chopped. Add the olive oil through the feed tube and process until smooth. Season with salt and pepper.

---

2 garlic cloves
1/3 cup chopped onion
2 tablespoons butter
2 tablespoons olive oil
16 ounces uncooked orzo
2 cups beef broth
1/2 teaspoon powdered saffron
Salt and pepper to taste
2 cups beef broth

ORZO: Combine the garlic and onion in a mini-food processor and process until minced. Heat the butter and olive oil in a 4-quart saucepan. Add the onion and garlic and sauté until the onion is tender. Add the orzo and sauté lightly, stirring to coat evenly. Add 2 cups beef broth and the saffron; season with salt and pepper. Bring to a boil and cook for 5 to 10 minutes or until most of the liquid is absorbed, stirring constantly. Add 2 cups beef broth and simmer, covered, for 15 minutes longer or until the orzo is tender and most of the liquid is absorbed, stirring frequently. Serve with the pesto.

PENNE WITH MUSTARD AND CHIVES

SERVES 6 TO 8

*Patricia Wells provided the inspiration for this recipe. Her book is a
compilation of recipes from some of her favorite restaurants in France.
You can see the French influence in this pasta dish with the addition of
Dijon mustard and chives, which make it unusual and delicious.*

5 quarts water
3 tablespoons kosher salt
8 ounces uncooked penne
1 cup heavy cream
2 tablespoons Dijon mustard
Sea salt or kosher salt to taste
Freshly ground white pepper
   to taste
1 cup chopped fresh tomato

Bring the water to a boil in a 6-quart pasta pot. Add
3 tablespoons kosher salt and the pasta and stir to
prevent sticking. Cook for 10 minutes or until tender
but still firm to the touch. Combine the cream and Dijon
mustard in a large saucepan and whisk to blend. Season
with sea salt and white pepper. Drain the pasta and add
to the saucepan with the tomato; toss to coat evenly. Let
stand, covered, for 1 to 2 minutes to absorb the sauce.

3 tablespoons finely minced
   fresh chives
Freshly grated Parmigiano-
   Reggiano cheese

TO SERVE: Spoon the pasta onto warmed serving plates,
into individual bowls or a large bowl. Garnish with the
chives and Parmigiano-Reggiano cheese. Serve as a first
course or a side dish.

HOMINY HASH

SERVES 6

*It would be hard for me, as a Texan, not to include a hominy dish. This is
great served with fried catfish or chicken and grilled ribs.*

1/4 cup olive oil
2 garlic cloves, minced
1 bunch green onions, chopped
1 yellow squash, cut into
   1/2-inch pieces
1 serrano chile, minced
1/4 cup all-purpose flour
1 (3-ounce) can yellow hominy
1 (15-ounce) can black-eyed peas
Chicken broth
1 red bell pepper
1/3 cup chopped cilantro
Salt and pepper to taste

Heat the olive oil in a 3-quart sauté pan. Add the garlic,
green onions, squash and serrano chile. Sauté until the
vegetables are tender. Add the flour and cook for 1 to
2 minutes, stirring to incorporate the flour completely.
Add the undrained hominy and black-eyed peas. Cook
until thickened, adding chicken broth if needed for
the desired consistency. Place the red bell pepper on a
baking sheet and roast under the broiler until charred
on all sides. Wrap in a paper towel and cool. Peel and
chop the pepper, discarding the seeds and membranes.
Add the pepper and cilantro to the hominy mixture.
Season with salt and pepper. Serve hot.

GRITS SOUFFLÉ RING

SERVES 6 TO 8

It is interesting to know that grits, cornmeal, and polenta are interchangeable. Yellow cornmeal can be used in this recipe and will taste like grits. It will unmold easily and can be filled with such wonderful concoctions as succotash.

2 cups milk

2 cups water

1¹⁄₂ cups uncooked grits or
   yellow cornmeal

1 teaspoon salt

¹⁄₄ cup (¹⁄₂ stick) butter, melted

1 cup (4 ounces) shredded
   Cheddar cheese

Chopped parsley to taste

¹⁄₄ teaspoon cayenne pepper

1 (4-ounce) can chopped
   green chiles

Salt and pepper to taste

3 egg yolks

3 egg whites

Grated Parmesan cheese

GRITS: Bring the milk and water to a boil in a saucepan and reduce the heat. Add the grits and 1 teaspoon salt and simmer until thickened, stirring frequently. Stir in the butter, Cheddar cheese, parsley, cayenne pepper and green chiles. Season with salt and black pepper to taste. Cool slightly. Mix in the egg yolks one at a time.

Beat the egg whites until stiff but not dry. Fold into the grits mixture. Spray a 9-inch ring mold with nonstick cooking spray and sprinkle with Parmesan cheese. Spoon the grits mixture into the mold and sprinkle with additional Parmesan cheese. Bake for 40 to 45 minutes or until the top is puffed and brown. Let stand for 10 minutes.

TO SERVE: Loosen the soufflé from the mold with a knife and remove to a platter. Serve alone immediately or fill with your choice of vegetable mixture. You can also reheat in a 350-degree oven.

FRIED RICE

*The secret to fried rice is to use rice that has been
prepared at least one day before being stir-fried. This makes
the actual preparation very quick and uses something
you can keep on hand.*

2 cups uncooked white rice, or
    1 cup uncooked brown rice
    and 1 cup uncooked
    white rice
4 cups water
1/2 teaspoon salt

COOKED RICE: Combine the rice with the water and salt in a saucepan and stir. Bring to a boil and reduce the heat to medium-low. Cover the rice and simmer for 15 minutes or until steam holes appear in the surface and all the water is absorbed; remove from the heat. Let stand, covered for 15 to 30 minutes. Spoon into a bowl and chill in the refrigerator for up to 4 days.

1 tablespoon vegetable oil
Eggs, beaten (optional)
1 tablespoon soy sauce
1 tablespoon oyster sauce
Vegetable additions, such as
    scallions, peppers, celery,
    carrots, snow peas and/or
    beans sprouts (optional)
Cooked meat additions, such as
    shrimp, chicken or turkey
    (optional)

FRIED RICE: Heat a wok over high heat for 2 to 3 minutes. Add the vegetable oil and heat for several seconds. Add the rice and eggs and stir-fry until the rice is seared and the eggs are cooked through. Add the soy sauce and oyster sauce and stir-fry just until evenly coated. Remove to a bowl.

Add any of the additions that you prefer to the wok and stir-fry until done to taste. Add to the rice and toss to mix well. Serve immediately or reheat at 400 degrees for 10 to 15 minutes.

NOTE: *Too much soy sauce or oyster sauce can overpower the rice. It should be used sparingly to add flavor and color.*

Mexican Tomatillo Rice

*The method used here is the same one used to cook
regular Mexican rice. I have varied the dish by using tomatillos
instead of canned red tomatoes.*

---

8 to 10 tomatillos
4 cups chicken broth

TOMATILLO PURÉE: Peel and wash the tomatillos. Bring the chicken broth to a boil in a saucepan. Add the tomatillos and cook for 5 to 10 minutes or until they lose their bright green color; drain, reserving the chicken broth. Purée the tomatillos with 1/2 cup of the reserved chicken broth in a blender.

---

3 tablespoons vegetable oil
1 cup coarsely chopped onion
2 garlic cloves, minced
2 serrano chiles, seeded
   and chopped
2 cups uncooked rice
1 to 2 tablespoons vegetable oil
1 red bell pepper, chopped
Salt and pepper to taste

RICE: Heat 3 tablespoons vegetable oil in a large sauté pan. Add the onion, garlic and serrano chiles and sauté for 3 to 4 minutes. Add the rice and stir-fry until it begins to brown. Add the tomatillo purée and the remaining 3 1/2 cups reserved chicken broth; mix well. Bring to a boil and reduce the heat. Simmer, covered, for 20 minutes or until the liquid has been absorbed; do not stir.

   Heat 1 to 2 tablespoons vegetable oil in a small sauté pan. Add the red bell pepper and sauté for 5 minutes or until tender-crisp. Add to the rice and toss to mix well. Season with salt and pepper.

Chopped cilantro (optional)

TO SERVE: Toss the rice mixture with the cilantro and serve immediately or spoon into a baking dish and reheat at 400 degrees for 20 to 30 minutes to serve later.

RICE WITH PEAS AND CASHEWS

SERVES 6

*I always welcome colorful dishes to serve as accompaniments
to holiday meals, and this is a good example.
Changing the type of rice changes the character entirely.*

3 tablespoons olive oil
1 cup cashews
1/4 cup raisins
1/2 cup uncooked wild rice
2 cups uncooked white rice
4 cups water
1 teaspoon salt
1/4 cup (1/2 stick) butter
2 cups frozen peas, thawed
Salt and pepper to taste

Heat the olive oil in a small saucepan. Add the cashews and sauté until golden brown. Add the raisins and sauté for 30 seconds or just until puffed. Cook the wild rice using the package directions. Drain any excess water. Combine the white rice with the water and salt in a saucepan and bring to a boil. Reduce the heat and simmer, covered, for 25 minutes or until the water is absorbed. Add the butter and mix well. Combine the wild rice, white rice and sautéed cashews and raisins in a bowl. Add the peas and mix gently. Season with salt and pepper and serve.

SIMPLE GRILLED POLENTA

SERVES 4 TO 6

*I first taught polenta in 1987 at the King Ranch in south Texas
where I had been invited to teach at a family summer camp. The dishes
included various ways to prepare native game birds, and polenta
made with yellow cornmeal was the accompaniment to Mexican Doves.*

6 cups water
1 tablespoon butter
1 bay leaf
1 (heaping) tablespoon salt
2 cups cornmeal
2 tablespoons olive oil
2 tablespoons butter

Combine the water, 1 tablespoon butter, the bay leaf and salt in a saucepan and bring to a boil. Reduce the heat to a simmer. Stir in the cornmeal gradually. Reduce the heat to low and cook until the mixture is smooth and thick, stirring constantly. Process in a food processor if necessary to remove any lumps. Discard the bay leaf and spoon into a buttered 8×13-inch dish. Cool to room temperature. Cut the mixture into rounds with a cutter. Heat the olive oil and 2 tablespoons butter in a grill pan until very hot. Add the polenta rounds and cook until brown on both sides. Serve immediately or reheat on a baking sheet at 400 degrees for 5 to 10 minutes.

POLENTA CUPS WITH WILD MUSHROOMS

MAKES 10 TO 12

*Polenta is an extremely versatile starch. It can be
served creamy or allowed to firm up and cut into shapes.
A new twist is to bake polenta in muffin tins to form
cups for holding a variety of fillings.*

1 ounce dried wild mushrooms
1 cup boiling water
2 tablespoons olive oil
1 cup chopped onion
2 garlic cloves, chopped
3 cups chopped fresh
   wild mushrooms
1/4 cup marsala
2 tablespoons chopped parsley
1/2 cup heavy cream
Salt and pepper to taste
1 teaspoon beef extract

WILD MUSHROOM FILLING: Combine the dried mushrooms with the hot water in a small bowl and let stand for 10 minutes to reconstitute; drain and press to remove the excess moisture, reserving the soaking liquid. Chop the mushrooms.

    Heat the olive oil in a 3-quart saucepan over medium heat. Add the onion and garlic and sauté until the onion is tender. Add the fresh mushrooms and sauté for 5 to 10 minutes or until the mushrooms are tender. Stir in the marsala, parsley, reconstituted mushrooms and the reserved mushroom soaking liquid. Cook until most of the liquid evaporates. Stir in the cream and season with salt, pepper and beef extract. Cook until thickened to the desired consistency.

3 cups water
1 teaspoon salt
1 cup polenta
1 teaspoon dried thyme
1 cup (4 ounces) grated
   Parmesan cheese
Salt and pepper to taste

POLENTA CUPS: Combine the water and 1 teaspoon salt in a saucepan and bring to a boil. Whisk in the polenta and thyme gradually and cook for 5 minutes or until thick, stirring constantly. Stir in the Parmesan cheese and season with salt and pepper. Drop 1 large tablespoonful of the warm polenta into 10 to 12 buttered muffin cups; let cool slightly. Press an indentation in the center to form the cups.

TO FINISH AND SERVE: Chill until ready to bake or bake immediately at 400 degrees for 10 minutes. Let cool slightly, then unmold the cups onto a serving platter. Fill with hot mushroom mixture.

CREAMY GARLIC POLENTA WITH MASCARPONE

SERVES 5 TO 8

I served this dish with sea bass at a dinner party in 2005. It is also a wonderful accompaniment for quail or any roasted meat.

3 whole garlic bulbs
1/4 cup olive oil
8 cups (or more) chicken broth
2 cups cornmeal
8 ounces mascarpone cheese
1 cup heavy cream
1/4 cup chopped parsley
Salt and pepper to taste
Butter (optional)

Sprinkle the garlic with the olive oil and wrap in foil. Roast at 400 degrees for 40 minutes or until tender. Cut off the tops of the cloves with kitchen shears and squeeze the roasted garlic into a bowl.

Bring the chicken broth to a boil in a large stockpot and reduce the heat to medium. Whisk in the cornmeal gradually. Cook until creamy, stirring frequently and adding additional chicken broth if needed for the desired consistency. Stir in the roasted garlic, mascarpone cheese, cream and parsley. Season with salt and pepper and stir in butter.

Chopped parsley

TO SERVE: Spoon into a serving dish and top with parsley to serve immediately or reheat with additional cream or broth to serve later.

NOTE: *One part cornmeal to three parts liquid is the usual ratio for polenta, but you will need more liquid if the polenta is to be served very creamy.*

Risotto

*I have tried many variations of risotto to serve
with duck confit and found that the simpler ingredients the
better. This basic recipe uses only a little shallot and
chicken broth and makes a wonderful mild risotto that is the perfect
base for duck confit, vegetable risotto, or mushroom
risotto. Serve it as an accompaniment, as a main course with
a salad, or as a first course.*

4 cups (or more) chicken broth
1 tablespoon olive oil
1 shallot, finely chopped
1 cup uncooked arborio rice
1/2 cup white wine
Salt and pepper to taste
1/4 cup heavy cream
2 to 3 tablespoons grated
   Parmesan cheese

Bring the chicken broth to a boil in a saucepan over high heat. Reduce the heat to medium and maintain the broth at a simmer.

Heat the olive oil in a heavy saucepan over medium heat. Add the shallot and sauté for 2 minutes or until tender. Add the rice and sauté lightly until evenly coated. Add the wine and cook until the wine is absorbed, stirring constantly.

Add the simmering broth 1/2 cup at a time and cook until the liquid is absorbed after each addition, stirring constantly until all the broth is used and the mixture is creamy, about 18 to 20 minutes total cooking time. Add water and continue to cook if the rice is not tender by the time all the broth has been absorbed. Season with salt and pepper. Stir in the cream and Parmesan cheese just before serving.

Duck Confit (page 109)
   (optional)
Sautéed mushrooms or
   vegetables (optional)
Chopped parsley

TO FINISH AND SERVE: Stir in Duck Confit and sautéed wild mushrooms and heat to serving temperature. Spoon onto serving plates and garnish with parsley.

NOTE: You can prepare the risotto in advance, leaving it slightly undercooked and finish it with the last of the chicken broth, cream, and Parmesan cheese just before serving.

Ricotta Cheese Bread

Serves 8 to 10

The ricotta in the batter makes this into a smooth bread with very few holes. It is great fresh out of the oven, but I especially like it sliced and toasted. When nicely browned on both sides, the outside is crisp, but the inside is still soft. It is a great companion to soups, salads, or light suppers. The herbs can be varied to make it unique each time you bake it.

1/2 to 2/3 cup lukewarm milk
1 tablespoon sugar
1 envelope dry yeast
6 tablespoons butter, melted
  and cooled
2 eggs, at room temperature
2 teaspoons salt
1 1/2 cups ricotta cheese
1 to 2 tablespoons chopped
  fresh basil and rosemary
5 cups (or more) unbleached
  flour
1 egg
1 tablespoon water

BREAD: Combine the milk and sugar in a measuring cup and sprinkle the yeast over the surface. Let stand for 3 to 4 minutes or until bubbly. Combine the butter with 2 eggs and salt in a food processor fitted with a steel blade; process until smooth. Add the ricotta cheese, basil and rosemary; process for 30 seconds or until well mixed. Add the yeast mixture and mix well.

Add 3 cups of the flour and process until the flour is incorporated; the dough will be wet. Place 1 cup of the remaining flour on a pastry cloth and spoon the dough onto the cloth. Sprinkle the remaining 1 cup flour on top and knead the dough for 8 to 10 minutes or until the dough forms a smooth ball that is not sticky, adding additional flour if necessary. Place the dough in a large bowl sprayed with nonstick cooking spray, turning to coat the surface. Let rise, covered, for 1 1/2 hours or until doubled in bulk. Punch down the dough and shape in a smooth loaf in a 5×9-inch loaf pan sprayed with nonstick cooking spray. Let rise for 30 minutes.

Beat 1 egg with the water in a small bowl. Brush on the dough. Bake at 375 degrees for 50 minutes or until the top is golden brown and the loaf sounds hollow when tapped.

Butter

To SERVE: Slice the bread and spread with butter. Wrap in foil and reheat at 375 degrees. You can also spread one side with butter and broil on both sides until golden brown.

NOTE: I have two main rules to ensure success when baking bread. The first is to be sure that the liquid in which you proof the yeast is lukewarm rather than hot. The second is to add salt. If you forget the salt, you might as well throw the bread out; it will have no flavor.

WHOLE GRAIN FENNEL FLATBREAD

MAKES 1 THIN LOAF

*I cannot remember when I was first introduced to this wonderful
flatbread, but I think it originated with Madeleine Kamman. I spent ten
days studying with her in Annecy, France. I remember that she
used lots of fennel, so I believe that this is one of her creations. It is one
of the most popular breads that I have taught.*

1 package dry yeast
1/4 cup lukewarm water
2 cups bread flour
1 cup whole wheat flour
1/2 cup hard winter wheat
1 tablespoon fennel seeds
1 1/2 teaspoons salt
1/2 to 3/4 cup water
1/3 cup olive oil
Coarse salt

Dissolve the yeast in 1/4 cup lukewarm water in a
cup and let stand until bubbly. Mix the bread flour,
whole wheat flour and winter wheat in a mixing bowl.
Make a well in the center and add the yeast, fennel
seeds, 1 1/2 teaspoons salt and 1/2 cup water, or enough
to bind the mixture. Knead on a floured surface for
10 minutes. Place in a bowl oiled with olive oil and
turn to coat the surface. Let rise, covered, for 1 1/2 hours
or until doubled in bulk. Knead in 1/3 cup olive oil
and pat into an oval on a baking sheet. Make nine
indentations in the dough. Brush with olive oil and
sprinkle with coarse salt. Bake at 350 degrees for
30 minutes or until golden brown.

CORN BREAD TERRINE WITH MUSHROOMS AND CORN

SERVES 8 TO 10

*I am always looking for new ways to present "dressing" at a holiday
table. This method is different and elegant. The terrine is
easily baked in a loaf pan, but has to be inverted to unmold, making
it hard to keep the pretty crunchy side intact. It is more
easily ccomplished in a springform pan, as I have done here.*

2 tablespoons butter
8 ounces mushrooms, chopped
1 bunch green onions, chopped
4 ribs celery, chopped
2 red bell peppers, chopped
3 garlic cloves, minced
1/2 cup chopped parsley
1 teaspoon dried thyme
1 teaspoon dried sage
8 ounces fresh corn kernels
2 (8-ounce) cans sliced water
    chestnuts, drained
3 packages yellow
    corn bread mix
2 to 3 cups chicken broth
Salt and pepper to taste
1/4 cup (1/2 stick) butter
2 eggs
Butter

BREAD: Melt 2 tablespoons butter in a large sauté pan.
Add the mushrooms, green onions, celery, red bell
peppers and garlic; sprinkle with the parsley, thyme
and sage. Sauté until tender-crisp. Add the corn and
sauté for 1 to 2 minutes. Stir in the water chestnuts.

Prepare the corn bread using the package directions.
Crumble the corn bread and reserve 2 cups of the
crumbs. Add the remaining crumbs to the vegetable
mixture and mix well.

Add the chicken broth to the vegetable mixture
and cook over medium heat until moistened, adding
additional chicken broth if needed for the desired
consistency. Season with salt and pepper and add
1/4 cup butter. Cool the mixture to room temperature
and add the eggs; mix well. Spoon into an 8- to 10-inch
springform pan.

Spread the reserved corn bread crumbs on a baking
sheet and toast at 350 degrees for 10 to 15 minutes or
until crisp. Sprinkle over the terrine and press firmly
into the mixture. Dot with additional butter. Bake at
350 degrees for 30 to 40 minutes or until the top
is brown.

Watercress or Italian parsley
Cranberries or kumquats

TO SERVE: Place the springform pan on a serving
plate and remove the side of the pan. Garnish with
watercress and cranberries.

Desserts and Sweets

Almond Crunch Cake (recipe on page 198)

BLACK PLUM TARTS

*This is a simpler version of the Black Plum Tart found in the
12 Seasons Cookbook by Alfred Portales, chef at the Gotham Bar and
Grill in New York City in 2001. One unusual variation is to use a
variety of plums and vary the mixture of plum types among the tarts in
the batch. The color and taste of each type of plum is slightly
different and makes for an interesting presentation, especially if you
alternate black and red plum slices. Remember that
plums are at their best in the summer.*

**1 package frozen puff
  pastry, thawed**

TART PASTRY: Roll the puff pastry dough into a rectangle
1/4 inch thick. Cut into eight circles with a 33/4-inch
cutter, rerolling the dough if necessary. Place on a
ungreased baking sheet and prick with a fork.

**8 black plums or a variety of
  plums, peeled and pitted
2 to 4 tablespoons brown sugar
2 tablespoons granulated sugar
1/4 cup (1/2 stick) butter,
  chopped**

TART: Slice the plums into 1/4-inch wedges. Fan the
slices in a circle on the pastry rounds and sprinkle
with the brown sugar and granulated sugar. Dot with
the butter. Bake at 250 degrees for 20 to 25 minutes
or until the plums are tender and the pastry is crisp.

Ginger Ice Cream (page 217)

TO SERVE: Serve hot or warm with a scoop of ginger
ice cream.

*VARIATION: This general recipe can be used with any
fruit. To use Golden Delicious apples, mix 5 tablespoons
suga, 2 tablespoons minced crystallized ginger and
2 tablespoons lemon juice and toss it with the apples.
Arrange the apples on a large pâte brisée pastry.
Top with additional sugar and butter and brush with
apricot jam when it comes from the oven.*

NOTE: It is even easier to make this as one large tart.

Black Plum Tarts

Individual Chocolate Soufflés with Caramel Sauce

Serves 8 to 10

Don't be scared of serving soufflés to company because you think they need to be finished at the last minute. This soufflé can be fully prepared a day in advance and stored in the refrigerator. It can then just be popped into a preheated oven and voilá—instant dessert.

3/4 cup sugar
6 tablespoons corn syrup
1/4 cup water
Pinch of salt
1/2 cup heavy cream
1/2 teaspoon vanilla extract

CARAMEL SAUCE: Combine the sugar, corn syrup, water and salt in a heavy saucepan and mix well. Bring to a boil, stirring constantly to dissolve the sugar. Boil until the mixture is a golden caramel color. Remove from the heat and add the cream and vanilla. Stir for 1 minute to mix well. Cool to room temperature; the sauce will thicken as it cools. Store in the refrigerator for up to 3 weeks. Bring to room temperature before serving.

1/3 cup sugar
6 tablespoons butter
1/3 cup heavy cream
8 ounces fine-quality
　bittersweet chocolate,
　finely chopped
4 large egg yolks
7 egg whites
1/4 teaspoon cream of tartar
Pinch of salt
1/4 cup sugar

SOUFFLÉS: Spray six 1-cup ramekins with nonstick cooking spray and coat with 1/3 cup sugar, shaking out any excess sugar. Melt the butter in a small saucepan over low heat. Add the cream and bring just to a boil; remove from the heat. Add the chocolate and stir until the chocolate melts and the mixture is smooth. Cool until the mixture is not hot to the touch. Stir in the egg yolks one at a time.

　Beat the egg whites with the cream of tartar and salt in a bowl until stiff peaks form. Add 1/4 cup sugar gradually, beating constantly just until combined. Fold 1/4 of the egg whites into the chocolate mixture. Fold in the remaining egg whites. Spoon into the prepared ramekins and smooth the tops with a knife. Run the tip of the knife around the edges of the soufflés to aid in rising. Store, covered with plastic wrap, in the refrigerator for up to 24 hours or bake immediately.

TO FINISH AND SERVE: Place the ramekins on a baking sheet and place in the upper third of a 375-degree oven. Bake for 20 minutes or until the soufflés puff and the surfaces crack. Serve with the caramel sauce.

VINCENT PRICE'S DIANA TORTE

SERVES 10 TO 12

My love of cooking began when I was newly married.
I had never really cooked before, and turning out dishes became
almost magical to me. Several other friends who felt this
way joined me in forming a gourmet club. This was one of my first
attempts as a club member. It is an extremely easy recipe
with knock-out results. It comes directly from Vincent Price's
classic cookbook, one of my all-time favorites.

---

28 coconut macaroons, crushed

1 quart chocolate ice cream,
　slightly softened

2 tablespoons chocolate
　fudge sauce

1 quart coffee ice cream,
　slightly softened

2 tablespoons chocolate
　fudge sauce

14 pieces of English
　toffee, crushed

TORTE: Sprinkle half the crushed macaroons in the bottom of an oiled 8-inch springform pan. Press down firmly to make a smooth layer. Spread the chocolate ice cream evenly over the macaroon layer and drizzle with 2 tablespoons chocolate fudge sauce. Sprinkle with the remaining macaroons and spread the coffee ice cream over the top. Drizzle with 2 tablespoons chocolate fudge sauce and sprinkle with the toffee. Freeze for 4 to 5 hours or until firm.

Chocolate fudge sauce

TO SERVE: Place the torte on a serving platter and remove the side of the springform pan. Let stand at room temperature for 30 minutes before serving. Cut into wedges to serve and pass with additional chocolate fudge sauce.

NOTE: To keep this dish easy to make, I suggest buying a good quality chocolate fudge sauce instead of making the sauce.

CHOCOLATE CHERRY CHARLOTTES WITH GRAND MARNIER CRÈME ANGLAISE

SERVES 6

The idea for this dessert came from Gourmet magazine.
I love the pairing of dried sour cherries and chocolate. It is nice to know
that it can be assembled the night before and baked immediately
before serving. The Grand Marnier Crème Anglaise is a basic French
sauce using Grand Marnier instead of the traditional vanilla.
It finishes the dish off perfectly.

1/2 **vanilla bean, split**
1 **cup milk**
1 **cup heavy cream**
6 **egg yolks**
1/2 **cup sugar**
1 **tablespoon Grand Marnier**
   or kirsch

GRAND MARNIER CRÈME ANGLAISE: Scrape the seeds from the vanilla bean into a small saucepan with the milk and cream. Add the vanilla pod and heat just until scalded; do not boil. Beat the egg yolks with the sugar in a mixing bowl until very thick and lemon-colored. Add the hot mixture gradually, whisking constantly. Return to the saucepan and cook over medium heat for 3 to 6 minutes or until thick enough to coat the back of the spoon, stirring constantly. Remove the vanilla bean pod and stir in the Grand Marnier. Chill, covered, in the refrigerator.

2/3 **cup dried sour cherries**
1/4 **cup kirsch**
2 **tablespoons sugar**
2 **or 3 drops of almond extract**
1/2 **cup heavy cream**
31/2 **ounces bittersweet**
   chocolate, chopped
Pinch of salt
1 **tablespoon butter**

CHOCOLATE AND CHERRY FILLING: Combine the dried cherries, kirsch and sugar in a small saucepan and mix well. Bring to a boil, stirring occasionally to dissolve the sugar. Remove from the heat and let stand, covered, for 15 minutes. Stir in the almond extract.

Combine the cream, chocolate and salt in a small heavy saucepan. Cook over low heat for 3 minutes or until the chocolate is melted, stirring to blend well. Remove from the heat and stir in the butter until melted. Add the cherry mixture and mix well. Spoon into a metal bowl and freeze for 21/2 hours or until firm but not frozen solid.

1½ loaves challah or large
   brioche, sliced ½-inch thick
6 tablespoons unsalted butter,
   softened

CHARLOTTES: Cut twelve circles from the bread slices with a 1½-inch biscuit cutter. Cut forty-two rectangles from the trimmings and the remaining slices. Spread one side of each circle and rectangle with the butter. Place six circles buttered side down in six individual molds. Line the sides of each mold with five to seven of the rectangles, placing the vertical buttered sides out and slightly overlapping, pressing them to adhere to the molds. Trim any overhang flush with the tops of the molds.

Spoon the chocolate and cherry filling evenly into the prepared molds and top with the six remaining circles buttered sides up, pressing gently to fit. Place on a baking sheet and set on the middle rack in a 350-degree oven. Bake for 25 minutes or until the top is golden brown. Cool for 5 minutes.

Cherry jam

TO SERVE: Place individual serving plates over each charlotte and invert onto the plates. Spoon the Grand Marnier crème anglaise around the charlottes and dot with cherry jam.

Dark Chocolate and White Chocolate Mousse

Serves 14

I discovered this recipe in the San Antonio newspaper.
It is supposedly the chocolate mousse from L'Etoile, a local restaurant.
The original recipe was extremely confusing, but I have worked
with it to create a dish that is time consuming, but not difficult to make.
The good news is that it can be prepared several days in advance.
The two layers of chocolate are made in exactly the same manner,
and the dark layer can be prepared while the white layer is chilling.
The amounts given fill two to three loaf pans. Chocolate is sold
in grams, so don't let the measurement put you off.

---

250 grams white chocolate, broken into small pieces
1/4 cup cold water
1 envelope unflavored gelatin
3/4 cup heavy cream
8 egg whites

WHITE CHOCOLATE MOUSSE: Place the white chocolate in the top of a double boiler and melt over slightly simmering water, stirring until smooth. Place 1/4 cup cold water in a measuring cup. Sprinkle the gelatin over the water. Let stand for 3 minutes. Heat the cream in a saucepan until scalded. Remove from the heat and add the gelatin mixture, stirring until the gelatin dissolves completely. Cool slightly. Combine with the white chocolate in a bowl and mix well.

Beat the egg whites in a mixing bowl until firm but not dry. Fold several large tablespoonfuls into the white chocolate mixture, then fold the white chocolate mixture into the egg whites; do not overmix. Spoon the mixture evenly into two or three loaf pans, filling no more than half full. Chill in the refrigerator for 30 minutes.

---

250 grams bittersweet chocolate, broken into small pieces
1/4 cup cold water
1 envelope unflavored gelatin
3/4 cup heavy cream
8 egg whites

DARK CHOCOLATE MOUSSE: Prepare the dark chocolate layer in the same manner as the white chocolate layer, substituting bittersweet chocolate for the white chocolate. Spoon the mixture over the chilled white chocolate layer and chill until firm.

Crème Anglaise, chocolate sauce and/or raspberry sauce

TO SERVE: Dip the loaf pans into hot water for several seconds until you see the mousse loosen. Unmold onto a serving platter or cut into serving pieces and place on individual serving plates. Serve with crème anglaise, chocolate sauce and/or raspberry sauce.

GINGERSNAP CANNOLI WITH BLUEBERRY LIME FILLING AND MANGO SAUCE

MAKES 32, SERVES 8

*Never having made cannoli shells, I became curious about them.
This recipe is the combination of many different attempts to create a great
dessert cannoli. I have chosen one similar to a French lace cookie
flavored with ginger. It is not a typical cannoli, which makes it quite exciting.*

---

1 (28-ounce) can mangoes

MANGO SAUCE: Process the undrained mangoes in a food processor until smooth. Store in the refrigerator.

1/2 cup sugar
1/2 cup (1 stick) unsalted butter
1/2 cup dark corn syrup
2 teaspoons ground ginger
1 cup all-purpose flour

CANNOLI SHELLS: Combine the sugar, butter, corn syrup and ginger in a small saucepan. Cook until the sugar dissolves and butter melts, stirring to blend well. Bring to a boil and remove immediately from the heat. Stir in the flour all at once. Drop 1 teaspoon of the batter onto the four quarters of a heavy cookie sheet sprayed with nonstick cooking spray. Bake at 375 degrees for 2 to 3 minutes or until brown, watching carefully to prevent burning. Let stand for 15 to 30 seconds or just until the cookie begins to firm up. Remove from the baking sheet with a metal spatula and wrap immediately around cannoli forms. Repeat with the remaining batter.

1/2 cup sugar
Zest of 1 lime
16 ounces cream cheese, softened
8 ounces mascarpone cheese, softened
1/4 cup lime juice
1 teaspoon vanilla extract
Blueberries

BLUEBERRY LIME FILLING: Combine the sugar and lime zest in a food processor and process until minced. Add the cream cheese, mascarpone cheese and lime juice and process until smooth. Mix in the vanilla. Fold in blueberries.

Blueberries
Mint leaves or geranium blossoms

TO ASSEMBLE AND SERVE: Spoon the blueberry lime filling into a pastry bag and pipe into the cannoli shells or spoon the filling into the shells with a teaspoon. Place on serving plates and spoon the mango sauce around the cannoli. Sprinkle additional blueberries around the plate and garnish with a mint leaf or geranium.

191

Butterscotch Mousse Pie

Serves 8

Butterscotch seems like a "fall" flavor to me. In September,
however, it is still quite warm in many places. Thus we have created
a fall dessert that is still cold and refreshing. Double the
filling to make the dessert spectacular.

---

4 to 5 cups graham
   cracker crumbs
1/2 cup packed brown sugar
3/4 to 1 cup (1 1/2 to 2 sticks)
   butter, melted

GRAHAM CRACKER CRUST: Process the graham cracker crumbs and brown sugar in a food processor until combined. Pour the butter through the feed tube and process until moistened. Pat the crumb mixture into a 10-inch springform pan and bake at 350 degrees for 15 minutes. Cool on a wire rack.

2/3 cup packed dark
   brown sugar
2 tablespoons cornstarch
Pinch of salt
1 cup half-and-half
2 egg yolks
3 tablespoons butter
2 teaspoons vanilla extract

BUTTERSCOTCH FILLING: Whisk the brown sugar, cornstarch, salt and 1/2 cup of the half-and-half in a bowl until combined. Strain through a fine sieve into a medium saucepan using a rubber spatula to press out any lumps of sugar. Whisk in the remaining 1/2 cup half-and-half and the egg yolks. Cook over medium heat for 7 minutes or until thick and bubbly, stirring constantly. Remove from the heat and whisk in the butter 1 tablespoon at a time. Whisk in the vanilla until blended. Chill, covered with plastic wrap, for 3 hours or overnight.

---

2 cups heavy whipping cream
1/4 cup confectioners' sugar

TOPPING: Beat the whipping cream in a mixing bowl until soft peaks begin to form. Add the confectioners' sugar 1 tablespoon at a time, beating constantly until stiff peaks form.

1/2 cup Heath Bar Chips, or
   1/2 cup chopped peanuts

TO ASSEMBLE AND SERVE: Spread the butterscotch filling in the baked crust. Top with the topping, sealing to the edge. Sprinkle with the Heath Bar Chips. Store in the refrigerator until serving time. Place the springform pan on a platter or cake stand and remove the side. Slice and serve.

CHOCOLATE CHEESECAKE WITH ORANGE MILANO CRUST

SERVES 12 TO 14

Cheesecake is one of my favorite desserts. The most difficult part to me in baking cheesecake is avoiding overcooking it, which causes it to split. I have adapted this method for baking cheesecake from Cook Wise *by Shirley Corriher.*

1/2 package Pepperidge Farm
   Orange Milano cookies
1/2 (9-ounce) package
   chocolate wafers
1/4 cup (1/2 stick) butter, melted

ORANGE MILANO CRUST: Process the cookies and wafers in a food processor until coarsely chopped. Combine with the butter in a bowl and toss with a fork. Press over the bottom of a 9 1/2-inch springform pan sprayed with nonstick cooking spray. Bake at 350 degrees for 10 minutes. Cool to room temperature.

---

12 ounces semisweet chocolate
1/2 cup (1 stick) butter,
   chopped
24 ounces cream cheese,
   softened
1 cup sugar
Juice of 1 orange
1 tablespoon Triple Sec or
   Grand Marnier
1 cup sour cream
3 eggs

CHEESECAKE: Combine the chocolate and butter in a double boiler and melt over simmering water, stirring to blend well. Maintain at room temperature. Beat the cream cheese and sugar at medium speed in a mixing bowl until light and fluffy. Beat in the orange juice, orange liqueur and sour cream. Add the eggs one at a time, mixing well after each addition. Add the chocolate mixture and mix well.

Spread the mixture in the Orange Milano crust and place the springform pan in a larger pan of hot water lined with a kitchen towel. Bake at 325 degrees for 40 to 45 minutes without opening the oven door. Turn off the oven and let the cheesecake stand in the closed oven for 1 hour; the center will still wiggle when you remove it from the oven. Let cool to room temperature and chill in the refrigerator for 8 hours or longer.

Sweetened whipped cream
Drained canned mandarin
   orange sections, candied
   oranges, chocolate leaves
   and/or chocolate curls

TO SERVE: Loosen the cheesecake from the side of the pan with a knife and place on a serving plate; remove the side of the pan. Decorate with whipped cream and orange sections, candied oranges, chocolate leaves and/or chocolate curls.

CREPES SUZETTE

SERVES 6 TO 8

*This timeless recipe was one of the first desserts I taught
when I began teaching in 1977. At that time, it was quite advanced,
for crepes were only served at upscale French restaurants.
Today Crepes Suzette are rarely served, and that is exactly why
they need to be reintroduced.*

---

1 cup all-purpose flour
2 small eggs
1¹/2 cups (about) milk
¹/2 tablespoon sugar
2 tablespoons melted butter
¹/2 tablespoon vanilla extract
¹/2 teaspoon salt

CREPE BATTER: Place the flour in a mixing bowl and make a well in the center. Add the eggs to the well and add 1¹/4 cups milk, whisking constantly until smooth. Add the additional ¹/4 cup milk or enough to make a batter the consistency of heavy cream. Stir in the sugar, butter, vanilla and salt. Spoon into a liquid measuring cup, leaving any liquid not absorbed by the batter.

---

¹/4 cup (¹/2 stick) butter, melted

COOKING THE CREPES: Rub the bottom of a crepe pan or small skillet with a paper towel dipped in the melted butter for the first crepe. You may not need to rebutter the pan after each crepe, but you can expect to throw out the first crepe; the second crepe will be good. Pour 2 to 4 tablespoons of the crepe batter into the prepared pan and swirl the pan to coat the bottom thinly and evenly. Cook just until the crepe is set and turn the crepe with a spatula. Cook on the other side until set but not brown. Remove to a plate. Repeat with the remaining batter and butter if needed, stacking on the plate; it is not necessary to place plastic wrap between the crepes.

---

¹/2 cup (1 stick) unsalted
  butter, softened
¹/4 cup sugar
Grated zest of 1 orange
¹/4 to ¹/3 cup orange juice
2 to 4 tablespoons
  Grand Marnier

ORANGE BUTTER: Combine the butter, sugar and orange zest in a food processor and process until smooth. Add as much orange juice as needed to make the desired consistency, processing constantly. Mix in the Grand Marnier.

1 tablespoon sugar
Grand Marnier

To Finish and Serve: Spread the lighter side of each crepe with the orange butter. Fold the buttered sides of the crepes in half and then in half again to form triangles. Rub a baking pan with some of the remaining orange butter and arrange the crepes in the pan. Sprinkle with the sugar and Grand Marnier. Heat in a 400-degree oven for 5 to 10 minutes or until heated through.

Variation: You can also flambé the crepes at the table if you prefer. Heat $^1/2$ to $^3/4$ cup Grand Marnier before adding it to the crepes in a flambé pan, then ignite the mixture. Let the flames subside before serving.

Piña Colada Mousse with French Lace Cookies, Coconut Sauce and Raspberry Coulis

Serves 10

*My fascination with this recipe began long ago. The use of
coconut milk gives the dish a wonderful tropical
flavor. I chose to teach it because the cone-shaped cups
are an exciting presentation for the mousse.*

1 cup sweetened pineapple juice

²/3 cup sugar

5 large egg yolks

¹/2 cup unsweetened
coconut milk

1 cup chilled heavy cream,
whipped to soft peaks

10 (¹/3-cup) cone-shaped
paper cups

MOUSSE: Combine the pineapple juice and sugar in a small saucepan and mix well. Simmer until reduced to ³/4 cup. Beat the egg yolks lightly in a bowl. Add half the heated juice mixture in a slow stream, whisking constantly. Whisk in the remaining juice. Return the mixture to the saucepan and cook until thickened to custard consistency, stirring frequently. Cool to room temperature. Fold in the coconut milk and whipped cream.

Place the cone-shaped paper cups in small glasses to hold them upright. Spoon the mousse mixture into the cups and freeze, covered, for 8 hours or longer.

1 cup whole milk

¹/2 cup unsweetened coconut
milk

¹/2 cup sugar

3 large egg yolks

2 to 3 tablespoons dark rum

COCONUT SAUCE: Combine the milk, coconut milk and sugar in a small saucepan and mix well. Bring to a boil, stirring to dissolve the sugar completely. Beat the egg yolks lightly in a bowl. Add the heated coconut milk gradually, stirring constantly. Return to the saucepan and cook until thickened, stirring constantly. Stir in the rum. Chill, covered, in the refrigerator.

**1 (10-ounce) package frozen
raspberries, thawed
Sugar to taste**

RASPBERRY COULIS: Process the raspberries in a food processor until smooth. Combine with sugar in a small saucepan. Cook until the sugar dissolves, stirring frequently. Cool to room temperature. Chill in the refrigerator.

**French Lace Cookies (page 221)
Pineapple leaves**

TO ASSEMBLE AND SERVE: Tear the paper cups gently from the frozen mousses and invert onto ten serving plates. Cut each mousse into thirds diagonally and place one French Lace Cookie between each section. Spoon the coconut sauce around the mousses and dot the sauce with the raspberry coulis. Draw a knife decoratively through the sauce and coulis and garnish with pineapple leaves.

ALMOND CRUNCH CAKE

SERVES 10 TO 12

*A dear friend shared this recipe with me years ago. The sponge cake
is a great recipe by itself, and the almond brittle topping is incredible.
The finished product produces a beautiful and glamorous cake.
Serve it for that special birthday or anniversary.*

1¹/2 cups sugar
¹/4 teaspoon instant coffee
  granules
¹/4 cup light corn syrup
¹/4 cup hot water
1 tablespoon sifted baking soda
1 to 2 cups sliced almonds

ALMOND BRITTLE TOPPING: Combine the sugar, coffee granules, corn syrup and water in a saucepan and mix well. Cook to 290 degrees on a candy thermometer, hard-crack stage. Remove from the heat and add the baking soda immediately, stirring vigorously just until the mixture appears blended and pulls away from the side of the pan. Stir in the almonds and pour immediately into an ungreased pan. Let stand until hard. Crush into coarse pieces with a rolling pin.

1¹/2 cups sifted all-purpose flour
³/4 cup sugar
8 egg yolks
¹/4 cup cold water
1 tablespoon lemon juice
1 teaspoon vanilla extract
8 egg whites
1 teaspoon cream of tartar
1 teaspoon salt
¹/4 cup sugar

CAKE: Sift the flour and ³/4 cup sugar into a mixing bowl and make a well in the center. Add the egg yolks, water, lemon juice and vanilla to the well and beat until smooth.

Beat the egg whites with the cream of tartar and salt in a mixing bowl until very soft peaks form. Add ³/4 cup sugar gradually, beating constantly until stiff peaks form. Fold in the flour mixture gently.

Spoon the batter into an ungreased 10-inch tube pan. Cut through the batter five or six times in a circular pattern with a knife to release any air bubbles. Bake at 350 degrees for 50 to 55 minutes or until the top springs back when lightly touched. Invert the tube pan and let stand for 1 hour or until cool. Remove the cake from the pan and split horizontally into three or four equal layers.

4 cups heavy whipping cream
$1/2$ cup confectioners' sugar
12 ounces fresh strawberries,
  sliced

WHIPPED CREAM FILLING AND FROSTING: Whip the cream in a mixing bowl until soft peaks form. Add the confectioners' sugar two tablespoons at a time, beating until the mixture forms peaks that do not slip in the bowl. Fold the sliced strawberries into half of the whipped cream for the filling. Reserve the remaining whipped cream for the frosting.

Sliced almonds
Whole Strawberries

TO ASSEMBLE AND SERVE: Place one cake layer on a cake stand or serving plate. Spread a portion of the whipped cream with strawberries over the cake and top with a second layer of cake. Add the remaining layers of cake, filling between the layers with the remaining whipped cream with strawberries. Frost the cake with the plain whipped cream. Sprinkle the almond brittle topping over the top of the cake and press over the side. Press sliced almonds in the spaces between the brittle. Arrange whole strawberries around the cake.

VARIATION: *Buy a commercial angel food cake to fill and frost using this recipe; top it off with the Almond Brittle for an easy and glamorous dessert.*

Cajeta Flan Cake

Serves 12 to 16

If ever a recipe demonstrates the true magic of cooking, it is this one.
The cake and flan are baked together, but at the end of the baking
period, the flan is perfectly set at the bottom. It is a traditional Mexican
cake that seems to be lost by many today. I discovered the recipe in
the San Antonio newspaper and feel it is one worth preserving.

1¹/2 cups sugar
¹/4 cup water
2 tablespoon white corn syrup

CARAMELIZED SUGAR: Combine the sugar, water and corn syrup in a saucepan. Heat until the sugar dissolves and the mixture is clear, stirring once or twice. Increase the heat to high and bring to a boil. Boil until the sugar begins to caramelize; do not stir after the mixture reaches a boil. Boil until the mixture is the desired color. Pour into a bundt pan.

---

4 eggs
1 (14-ounce) can sweetened
    condensed milk
1 (12-ounce) can
    evaporated milk

FLAN MIXTURE: Combine the eggs, sweetened condensed milk, evaporated milk and vanilla in a mixing bowl and beat until smooth.

---

1 (2-layer) package chocolate or
    yellow cake mix

CAKE: Prepare the cake mix using the package directions. Spread over the caramelized sugar in the bundt pan. Spoon the flan mixture carefully over the cake mix in the bundt pan. Place the bundt pan in a larger pan filled with water. Bake at 350 degrees for 1 hour. Remove the bundt pan from the water bath and let stand for 10 to 15 minutes. Invert the pan onto a cake plate and lift very slowly from the cake. Cool to room temperature and chilled until serving time.

1¹/2 cups heavy whipping
    cream
¹/4 cup cajeta
2 teaspoons sugar
1 teaspoon vanilla extract

CAJETA CREAM: Beat the cream in a mixing bowl until soft peaks form. Add the cajeta, sugar and vanilla and beat until well mixed. Decorate the cake with the cajeta cream, using a pastry bag if desired. Serve the cake cold.

NOTE: *You can prepare this in individual ramekins if you prefer. Cajeta can be found in most Mexican markets.*

CARROT CAKE

SERVES 10 TO 12

*I discovered this recipe when my children were small, and
made it an Easter tradition in our family. I baked
it in one large rabbit mold instead of three round cake pans.*

2 cups all-purpose flour
2 teaspoons baking powder
2 teaspoons baking soda
2 teaspoons cinnamon
1 teaspoon salt
4 eggs
1¹/₂ cups sugar
1¹/₂ cups vegetable oil
3 cups grated carrots
¹/₂ cup raisins
¹/₂ cup chopped pecans

CAKE: Sift the flour with the baking powder, baking soda, cinnamon and salt. Beat the eggs until frothy in a large bowl. Add the sugar gradually, beating constantly until light and lemon-colored. Beat in the vegetable oil gradually. Fold in the flour mixture in several batches. Fold in the carrots, raisins and pecans, mixing evenly. Spoon into three buttered and floured 8-inch round cake pans. Bake at 350 degrees for 30 minutes. Cool in the pans for several minutes and remove to a wire rack to cool completely.

32 ounces cream cheese,
   softened
1 cup (2 sticks) butter, softened
1 to 2 cups confectioners'
   sugar, or to taste
2 cups drained crushed
   pineapple
2 teaspoons vanilla extract

PINEAPPLE CREAM CHEESE FILLING AND FROSTING:
Combine the cream cheese, butter and confectioners' sugar in a mixing bowl or food processor and mix until smooth. Add the pineapple and vanilla and mix well.

TO ASSEMBLE: Split each cake layer horizontally into two layers. Spread the pineapple cream cheese filling and frosting between the layers and over the top and side of the cake. Store in the refrigerator until serving time. Bring to room temperature to serve.

CHOCOLATE TRUFFLE CAKE WITH RASPBERRY SAUCE AND CRÈME ANGLAISE

SERVES 8

I developed this recipe for a Valentine class. The recipe is baked in a springform pan. I then cut out small circles or hearts and frost them with chocolate for beautiful individual desserts. Arrange them at different heights on a three-tiered cake stand for an impressive buffet presentation.

---

11 to 12 ounces Valrhona or Lindt bittersweet chocolate, chopped
10 tablespoons unsalted butter, sliced
2/3 cup sugar
5 large egg yolks
5 large egg whites
1/3 cup all-purpose flour, sifted

CAKE: Melt the chocolate and butter with the sugar in a double boiler over simmering water, stirring to mix well; the sugar will not dissolve completely. Cool to room temperature and spoon into a large bowl. Whisk in the egg yolks one at a time. Beat the egg whites in a mixing bowl until soft peaks form.

Sift the flour over the chocolate mixture; add half the egg whites and fold in with a whisk. Fold in the remaining egg whites with a spatula. Spoon into a buttered 10-inch springform pan. Bake at 350 degrees for 30 to 45 minutes or until a tester inserted into the center comes out with moist crumbs. Cool in the pan on a wire rack. Store at room temperature in an airtight container for up to 2 days if desired.

---

1 cup milk
1 cup heavy cream
1/4 vanilla bean, split
1 teaspoon vanilla extract
6 egg yolks
1/2 cup sugar
1 teaspoon Grand Marnier

CRÈME ANGLAISE: Combine the milk and cream in a saucepan. Scrape the seeds from the vanilla bean into the cream mixture and add the pod to the saucepan. Stir in the vanilla extract. Heat just until the mixture is bubbly around the edge.

Beat the egg yolks with the sugar in a bowl until thick and lemon-colored. Whisk in a small amount of the hot cream mixture. Whisk in the remaining cream mixture gradually. Return to the heat and cook until thick enough to coat a wooden spoon, stirring constantly. Stir in the liqueur. Cover with plastic wrap and store in the refrigerator until serving time. Remove the vanilla pod to serve.

2 (12-ounce) packages frozen
   raspberries, thawed
2 to 3 tablespoons
   raspberry jelly
Juice of 1 lemon
1/2 to 1 cup sugar, or to taste

RASPBERRY SAUCE: Combine the raspberries with the raspberry jelly and lemon juice in a food processor and process until puréed. Combine the raspberry purée with the sugar in a saucepan and heat until the sugar dissolves and the mixture is smooth. Strain into a bowl and pour into a plastic squeeze bottle. Store in the refrigerator until serving time.

6 1/2 ounces Valrhona or Lindt
   bittersweet chocolate,
   chopped
1/4 cup (1/2 stick) butter, melted
1/2 cup heavy cream
1 teaspoon espresso granules
1 tablespoon Triple Sec or
   other orange liqueur
   (optional)

CHOCOLATE GANACHE: Melt the chocolate with the butter in a double boiler over simmering water; remove from the heat. Bring the cream and espresso granules just to a simmer in a small saucepan, stirring to dissolve the espresso. Add the cream mixture and liqueur to the chocolate mixture and stir until smooth. Keep warm. Any ganache not needed to frost the cakes can be stored in the refrigerator and reheated to serve as chocolate syrup.

1 1/2 pints fresh raspberries
Fresh mint

TO ASSEMBLE AND SERVE: Place the cake on a plate and remove the side of the pan. Cut the cake into eight wedges. Invert the wedges so the flat sides are up and place on a large rack over a large shallow drip pan, spacing at least 1 inch apart. Spoon enough of the warm chocolate ganache over each wedge to coat; let stand for 5 minutes. Scrape up the excess ganache from the drip pan into a bowl and spoon over the wedges again, coating evenly. Let stand at room temperature for 1 to 6 hours or until the ganache is set. Spoon the crème anglaise onto serving plates and place one cake wedge on each plate. Garnish with the raspberry sauce and top with fresh raspberries and fresh mint.

LEMON CURD LAYER CAKE

SERVES 8 TO 10

*For some reason, I do not teach many cakes, but this one is special
enough for a birthday or grand celebration. Lemon curd is easy to make
and worth the effort, as commercial versions do not measure up.*

6 egg yolks
1 cup sugar
1/2 cup fresh lemon juice
1 teaspoon grated lemon zest
Pinch of salt
3/4 cup (11/2 sticks) unsalted
    butter, cut into 1/2-inch pieces

LEMON CURD: Combine the egg yolks, sugar, lemon juice, lemon zest and salt in a double boiler. Cook over hot water until the mixture thickens enough to coat the back of a spoon, stirring constantly. Remove from the heat and add the butter. Return to the heat and cook over medium heat for 12 minutes or until the mixture boils and thickens, whisking constantly. Spoon into a bowl and chill in the refrigerator for 5 hours or longer.

11/4 cups lemon curd
4 to 6 tablespoons
    confectioners' sugar
3 cups heavy whipping
    cream, chilled

LEMON CURD WHIPPED CREAM FROSTING: Beat 11/4 cups lemon curd with the confectioners' sugar in a large mixing bowl just until smooth. Beat the whipping cream in a medium mixing bowl until firm peaks form. Fold into the lemon curd mixture one-third at a time. Chill in the refrigerator for 4 hours or longer.

1/2 cup sugar
Grated zest of 1 1/2 lemons
1 1/2 cups cake flour
2 1/2 teaspoons baking powder
3/4 teaspoon salt
4 large egg yolks
1/4 cup vegetable oil
1/4 cup orange juice
1 1/2 teaspoons grated
   lemon zest
3/4 cup lemon curd
8 large egg whites
1/4 teaspoon cream of tartar
1 cup sugar

CAKE: Butter and flour three 9-inch cake pans with 1 1/2-inch sides and line with baking parchment. Combine 1/2 cup sugar and the zest from 1 1/2 lemons in a mini-food processor and process until finely minced. Combine with the flour, baking powder and salt in a large bowl and whisk to mix well. Add the egg yolks, vegetable oil, orange juice, 1 1/2 teaspoons lemon zest and 3/4 cup lemon curd; mix well.

Beat the egg whites with the cream of tartar in a large mixing bowl and beat until soft peaks form. Add 1 cup sugar gradually, beating until the egg whites are stiff but not dry. Beat the batter with the same beaters and fold the egg whites into the batter one-third at a time.

Divide the batter evenly among the prepared pans. Bake at 350 degrees for 25 minutes or until a tester inserted into the center comes out clean. Cool in the pans on wire racks for 15 minutes and invert onto the racks. Remove the baking parchment and cool completely.

Thin lemon slices
Mint
Fresh strawberries

TO ASSEMBLE AND SERVE: Spread the lemon curd whipped cream frosting between the layers and over the top and side of the cake. Garnish with lemon slices, mint and/or strawberries.

VARIATION: You can add sliced strawberries between the cake layers, if desired.

Ginger Cake with Brown Sugar Icing

Serves 8 to 10

In the late 1990s, I took a group to New York City to study with Karen Lee, the best fusion teacher in the area. This cake is an adaptation of one of her recipes. My students assure me that it is one of their favorites.

1/3 cup fresh bread crumbs
3 cups sifted all-purpose flour
1 teaspoon baking powder
1 teaspoon baking soda
1 teaspoon ground cinnamon
1/2 teaspoon ground cloves
1/2 teaspoon ground nutmeg
1 tablespoon ground ginger
1 teaspoon salt
1 cup (2 sticks) butter, softened
1 cup packed dark brown sugar
1 cup molasses
3 eggs
1 cup boilng water

CAKE: Butter a heavy bundt pan generously and sprinkle with bread crumbs. Sift the flour with the baking powder, baking soda, cinnamon, cloves, nutmeg, ginger and salt. Cream the butter and brown sugar in a mixing bowl until light and fluffy. Beat in the molasses. Add the eggs one at a time, mixing well after each addition. Add the dry ingredients in three additions, alternating with the boiling water and mixing well.

Spoon into the prepared bundt pan and tap on the counter to settle evenly. Bake at 325 degrees for 50 minutes or until a fork comes out almost clean and the cake has not yet pulled away from the side of the pan.

2 cups packed light
  brown sugar
1/3 cup heavy cream
1/4 cup (1/2 stick) butter
1 teaspoon vanilla extract
1 teaspoon salt

BROWN SUGAR ICING: Combine the brown sugar and cream in a medium saucepan and mix well. Bring to a boil over low heat, stirring constantly. Boil for exactly 1 minute. Remove from the heat and stir in the butter. Add the vanilla and salt and mix well. Beat until creamy and slightly thickened.

TO FINISH AND SERVE: Cool the cake slightly and remove to a serving platter. Pour the warm icing over the warm cake. Serve immediately or reheat at 350 degrees for 10 minutes to serve. Serve with ice cream. You can also cut the cake into individual servings to reheat it and serve with additional icing.

CRÈME BRÛLÉE NAPOLEONS

SERVES 8

This is a great variation of crème brûlée. The egg yolks make it possible to cut it into sections, which are then layered between sheets of phyllo to make Napoleons.

1/2 cup milk
2 cups heavy cream
1/2 cup sugar
1 or 2 vanilla beans, split
9 egg yolks, at room temperature

CRÈME BRÛLÉE: Combine the milk, cream and sugar in a heavy saucepan and mix well. Scrape the seeds from the vanilla beans into the mixture and add the pods. Bring to a boil and turn off the heat. Cool to room temperature and discard the vanilla pods. Whisk in the egg yolks. Spoon into a 9×13-inch baking dish and place in a larger pan filled with hot water. Bake at 300 degrees for 45 minutes or until set. Cool to room temperature and store in the refrigerator for up to 2 days.

8 sheets phyllo dough
1/2 cup (1 stick) butter, melted
3/4 cup sugar
1 cup pecans, toasted
Confectioners' sugar

PECAN PASTRY: Unroll the phyllo dough and remove one sheet, leaving the remaining sheets covered. Place on a work surface and brush with some of the melted butter. Mix the sugar and pecans in a bowl and sprinkle some of the mixture over the phyllo. Repeat the process with the remaining phyllo, butter and pecan mixture. Cut into 4×4-inch squares and place on baking sheets lined with baking parchment. Bake at 300 degrees for 10 minutes or until golden brown. Sift confectioners' sugar over the squares and place the baking sheets under the broiler. Broil for 1 minute or until brown. Store in an airtight container until needed.

Dessert sauce of your choice

TO ASSEMBLE AND SERVE: Cut the crème brûlée into sections. Stack two layers of the crème brûlée between three pastry squares to form Napoleons, placing the top pastry square with the pecan side up. Place on serving plates and serve immediately with the sauce of your choice.

CHOCOLATE AND RASPBERRY NAPOLEONS

SERVES 6

Chocolate hearts are layered with raspberry semifreddo (Italian for half frozen) for this Valentine dessert. Serve it with a chocolate sauce, a raspberry sauce, or both. For other occasions, you can cut the chocolate layers into rectangles as you would for regular napoleons.

---

1 (16-ounce) package frozen raspberries, thawed
1/3 cup sugar
2 tablespoons raspberry jam

RASPBERRY PURÉE: Combine the raspberries with the sugar and raspberry jam in a food processor and process until puréed. Place in a saucepan and cook over low heat until the sugar dissolves. Remove and reserve 2/3 cup of the purée for the semifreddo. Strain and reserve the remaining purée.

---

4 egg yolks
1/2 cup light corn syrup
2 tablespoons kirsch
1/4 cup sugar
2/3 cup raspberry purée
3 egg whites
Sugar to taste
1 cup heavy whipping cream

RASPBERRY SEMIFREDDO: Combine the egg yolks, corn syrup, kirsch and 1/4 cup sugar in a double boiler and mix well. Cook over simmering water until the mixture thickens enough to leave a ribbon-like thread from the whisk, whisking constantly. Add 2/3 cup raspberry purée and mix well. Cool to room temperature.

Beat the egg whites in a mixing bowl until frothy. Add sugar to taste and beat until stiff peaks form. Beat the cream in a mixing bowl until firm peaks form. Fold in the egg whites and raspberry mixture. Spoon into a freezer pan large enough to make a layer 3/4 inch deep. Freeze for 4 hours or up to 3 days.

---

8 ounces bittersweet chocolate, chopped

CHOCOLATE HEARTS: Melt the chocolate in a double boiler or microwave. Spread in a thin layer on a nonstick baking mat. Place in the freezer for 4 to 6 minutes or until set. Cut into heart shapes with a cutter. Store in an airtight container in the freezer for up to 2 weeks.

Melted bittersweet chocolate

TO ASSEMBLE AND SERVE: Remove the semifreddo from the freezer no more than 10 minutes before serving, as it will not be frozen hard. Cut into hearts or other shapes the size of the chocolate. Stack two layers of the semifreddo between three layers of chocolate hearts to form the Napoleons. Place on serving plates and serve or freeze until serving time. Serve with the reserved raspberry purée and melted chocolate as sauces.

Toasted Coconut Pie

Serves 8

*This recipe came from a good friend and wonderful cook from Dallas.
We became friends through golf, but quickly discovered we had a
common interest in food. Every recipe she sends me is great, and several
are in this book. I served it to rave reviews at both Thanksgiving and
Christmas, but it is good in the summer as well.*

---

3 eggs
1½ cups sugar
½ cup (1 stick) butter, melted
¼ cup lemon juice
1 teaspoon grated lemon zest
1 teaspoon vanilla extract
1 unbaked pie shell

PIE: Whisk the eggs lightly in a bowl. Add the sugar, butter, lemon juice, lemon zest and vanilla. Beat for 5 minutes. Spoon into the pie shell and bake at 350 degrees for 40 to 45 minutes or until the crust is golden brown. Cool to room temperature on a wire rack.

---

1 (3-ounce) can flaked coconut
2 cups heavy whipping cream
3 tablespoons confectioners' sugar

TO FINISH AND SERVE: Toast the coconut in a 250-degree oven just until light brown, watching closely to prevent burning; do not use a toaster oven. Beat the cream in a mixing bowl until soft peaks form. Add the confectioners' sugar gradually, beating constantly until the cream is thick enough not to slip in the bowl. Spread the whipped cream over the pie at serving time and sprinkle with the coconut.

NOTE: I recommend the kind of commercial pie pastry that has to be slightly rolled out. Chill until time to fill. If you are a purist, you can prepare your own pie pastry from the recipe on page 215.

Whipped Kahlúa Pie

Serves 8

*I have hosted Christmas Day lunch at my house since
I was first married, almost forty years ago. It is a seated affair for about
thirty-five people. To accomplish this, all young relatives help me plate
the food and pass the soup and dessert. The dinner is served buffet-style,
and because of the hectic pace of the season, I select dishes that I
can prepare several days in advance. The dishes must also be easy to
prepare and something even small children will enjoy. This has
become my standard dessert for the occasion; it has an ice cream base
and can be frozen long before I need to serve it.*

½ to 1 (9-ounce) package
   chocolate wafers, crushed
6 tablespoons butter, melted
1 tablespoon sugar
½ cup finely chopped pecans

CHOCOLATE PECAN CRUST: Combine the wafer crumbs, butter, sugar and pecans in a bowl and mix well. Press into a 10-inch pie pan. Bake at 350 degrees for 10 minutes. Cool to room temperature.

2 cups heavy whipping cream
⅔ cup Kahlúa
1 teaspoon vanilla extract
4 Heath candy bars, crushed
1 quart coffee ice cream,
   softened

PIE FILLING: Whip the cream in a mixing bowl until soft peaks form. Add the Kahlúa and vanilla. Fold in the crushed candy bars and ice cream. Spread in the prepared crust and freeze until serving time.

12 ounces chocolate chips
1 cup heavy cream

CHOCOLATE SAUCE: Combine the chocolate and cream in a double boiler. Cook over simmering water until the chocolate melts, stirring to blend evenly. Spoon into a plastic squeeze bottle.

TO SERVE: Cut the pie into wedges and place on serving plates. Squeeze the chocolate sauce over the wedges in random patterns.

FROZEN PUMPKIN MOUSSE PIE

SERVES 10 TO 12

Fall is my favorite time of the year. In south Texas, we always imagine that it will be cool, with wonderful fall leaves. In reality, we are usually surrounded by pumpkins with weather that is quite warm. This pumpkin mousse puts one in the mood for fall, but it is a cold dessert, just perfect for our climate. Even those who do not love pumpkin will be won over by it. It is also a dessert that will take the stress out of the holidays, for it can be made up to a week in advance and frozen.

3 cups pecans, toasted and
    finely chopped
1/2 cup packed brown sugar
1/4 cup (1/2 stick) butter, melted

PECAN CRUST: Mix the pecans and brown sugar in a bowl. Add the butter and mix well. Press over the bottom and up the side of a 9-inch springform pan. Chill for 15 to 30 minutes. Bake at 350 degrees for 10 minutes or until golden brown. Cool to room temperature.

1 cup heavy cream
1 cup packed brown sugar
8 large egg yolks
1 1/2 cups canned pumpkin
1/2 cup light corn syrup
3 tablespoons dark rum
1 1/2 teaspoons ground ginger
1 teaspoon ground cinnamon
1/4 teaspoon ground nutmeg
1 1/2 cups heavy whipping cream

PIE FILLING: Combine 1 cup cream with the brown sugar and egg yolks in a heavy saucepan or double boiler; whisk until smooth. Cook over medium heat until very thick, stirring constantly. Beat in the pumpkin, corn syrup, rum, ginger, cinnamon and nutmeg. Beat 1 1/2 cups whipping cream in a mixing bowl until firm peaks form. Fold into the pumpkin mixture. Spoon into the pecan crust and freeze for 8 hours or longer.

1 to 2 cups pecan halves
1 jar butterscotch-caramel
    sauce
1 jar butterscotch-caramel
    sauce, heated

TO ASSEMBLE AND SERVE: Arrange the pecan halves on the top of the pie and top with 1 jar butterscotch-caramel sauce. Freeze until serving time. Place the pie on a serving plate and remove the side of the pan. Let stand at room temperature for 10 to 15 minutes. Cut into wedges and serve with the heated sauce.

Pumpkin Crème Brûlée Tart

Serves 8 to 10

Pumpkin Crème Brûlée Tart is one of my favorite
holiday desserts. The crème brûlée flavored with pumpkin can
also be baked without a crust in individual molds,
just as you would traditional crème brûlée.

1/2 cup (1 stick) butter,
   softened
6 tablespoons sugar
1 egg yolk
1 1/4 cups all-purpose flour
3/4 cup ground pecans
1/2 teaspoon ground nutmeg

PECAN TART SHELL: Cream the butter and sugar in a mixing bowl or food processor until light and smooth. Add the egg yolk, flour, pecans and nutmeg and process until crumbly. Press into a 10-inch pie plate sprayed with nonstick cooking spray. Bake at 375 degrees for 15 to 20 minutes or until the edge is light brown.

---

1 cup canned pumpkin
2 cups heavy cream
1/2 teaspoon ground cinnamon
1/4 teaspoon ground allspice
8 egg yolks
3/4 cup sugar
1 teaspoon vanilla extract

PUMPKIN CRÈME BRÛLÉE: Combine the pumpkin, cream, cinnamon and allspice in a saucepan. Heat until hot but not boiling, stirring constantly. Beat the egg yolks with the sugar in a bowl. Add 1/2 cup of the hot liquid to the egg yolk mixture and mix well. Add the remaining hot liquid in a slow stream, stirring constantly. Stir in the vanilla.

Spoon into the pecan tart shell and bake at 350 degrees for 25 to 30 minutes or just until set; do not overcook. Cool to room temperature and chill in the refrigerator for 8 hours or longer.

1/2 to 1 cup packed light
   brown sugar

TO FINISH AND SERVE: Sprinkle brown sugar generously over the top of the tart. Broil until the sugar is melted and brown. Cut into wedges and serve cold.

FRENCH APPLE TART WITH PECANS

SERVES 8 TO 10

*I first served this tart years ago at a Christmas buffet, where it
met with rave reviews. It is especially useful because it can be made in
advance and frozen if necessary. Let come to room temperature or reheat
slightly before serving. I credit the original recipe to Dean Fearing.*

1 refrigerator pie pastry
3 or 4 Granny Smith apples,
   peeled, cored and
   thinly sliced
4 large eggs
1 cup sugar
1 cup dark corn syrup
2 tablespoons melted butter
1 teaspoon vanilla extract
1/2 cup pecan pieces

APPLE TART: Roll the pie pastry as desired and fit into a 10-inch pie plate. Chill until time to fill. Arrange apple slices in one direction around the edge of the pie plate. Arrange a second circle of apples slices in the opposite direction inside the first circle.

Combine the eggs and sugar in a bowl and mix well. Add the corn syrup, butter and vanilla and mix until the sugar dissolves. Pour carefully over the apples without disturbing the arrangement. Sprinkle the pecans around the edge. Bake at 350 degrees for 1 to 1 1/2 hours or until set.

Ice cream (optional)

TO SERVE: Cool the tart slightly and cut into wedges. Serve with ice cream.

Mango Tarts

*Lime curd, mangoes, and macadamias are the main
ingredients in this dessert. Although they are fantastic tastes alone,
their flavors multiply when they are blended together.*

---

2 cups macadamia nuts
1¹/2 cups sweetened
    shredded coconut
¹/2 cup packed brown sugar
3 large egg whites

MACADAMIA COCONUT CRUST: Sprinkle the macadamia nuts on a baking sheet and roast at 200 degrees for 10 minutes or until light brown. Process in a food processor until crushed. Add the coconut, brown sugar and egg whites and process to form a ball. Pat into individual tart pans sprayed with nonstick cooking spray. Bake at 350 degrees for 10 to 15 minutes or until light brown.

---

1 cup sugar
³/4 cup lime juice
10 large egg yolks
Grated zest of 1 lime
¹/2 cup (1 stick) butter, sliced

LIME CURD: Combine the sugar, lime juice, egg yolks and lime zest in a heavy saucepan or double boiler. Cook until thick, stirring constantly; do not allow to boil. Remove from the heat and add the butter gradually, stirring to mix well after each addition. Spoon into the macadamia coconut crust and cover with plastic wrap. Place in the refrigerator until chilled and firm.

---

2 or 3 mangoes, sliced
¹/2 cup red currant jelly
2 tablespoons water
1¹/2 cups chopped macadamias
Mint leaves

TO ASSEMBLE AND SERVE: Arrange the mango slices on the top of the tarts in a pinwheel design with the ends meeting in the center. Heat the red currant jelly with the water in a small saucepan, stirring until smooth. Brush over the mangoes and tart shells. Sprinkle with the macadamia nuts and garnish with mint leaves.

VARIATION: You can substitute pistachios for the macadamia nuts used as topping and add a hint of green as well as a different flavor. You can also prepare this in a 10-inch tart pan with a removable bottom.

UPSIDE-DOWN PEAR TART

SERVES 6 TO 8

*What could be better than pears that are slowly caramelized,
covered with pastry, and baked in the oven? The dish doesn't look like
much when it is cooking, but when you invert it onto a serving platter,
you will find a perfect pear tarte Tatin every time.*

1 1/4 cups all-purpose flour
1/2 teaspoon salt
1/2 cup (1 stick) butter,
   cut into 8 pieces
1/3 cup cold water

TART PASTRY: Process the flour and salt in a food processor to mix well. Add the butter and pulse until the mixture resembles small peas. Add the water through the feed tube, processing constantly until the pastry forms a ball. Use immediately or wrap in plastic wrap and chill until needed.

1/4 cup (1/2 stick) butter
1/2 cup sugar
2 pounds (3 to 5) Bosc pears,
   peeled, cored and
   cut into halves
Ground cinnamon to taste

TART: Melt the butter in a 9- to 10-inch cast-iron skillet. Stir in the sugar. Arrange the pear halves with the wide portion toward the outside of the skillet and with the cut sides up. Sprinkle with cinnamon. Cook without stirring for 10 to 25 minutes until the sugar is a deep caramel color, shaking the skillet as needed to mix. Cool the mixture in the skillet.

Roll the pastry and place over the pears, tucking the edge around and under the pears. Bake at 425 degrees for 15 to 30 minutes or until the pastry is brown.

TO SERVE: Invert immediately onto a serving plate. Serve at room temperature with ice cream. You can also invert the tart onto an oven-proof plate and reheat at serving time.

LEMON-LIME MOUSSE WITH MIXED BERRIES AND MANGOES

SERVES 12

Here is a wonderful dessert to serve on a hot summer day.
Serve it as the finale for a Fourth of July celebration, using red and blue
berries against the white of the semifrozen mousse.

1½ cups sugar
8 large egg yolks
⅓ cup fresh lemon juice
⅓ cup fresh lime juice
5 tablespoons unsalted butter
2 teaspoons grated lime zest
2 cups heavy whipping cream,
　chilled

LEMON-LIME MOUSSE: Line a 12-cup ring mold with plastic wrap, allowing the plastic to overhang the edges by 3 inches. Combine the sugar, egg yolks, lemon juice, lime juice, butter and lime zest in a large metal bowl or double boiler. Place over simmering water without allowing the water to touch the bottom of the bowl or pan. Cook for 7 minutes or to 180 degrees on a candy thermometer, whisking constantly. Remove from the heat and beat for 8 minutes or until thick and cool.

Beat the whipping cream in a mixing bowl until firm peaks form. Fold into the cooked mixture. Spoon into the prepared mold and smooth the top. Cover with the plastic wrap and freeze for 8 hours to 1 week.

12 ounces fresh strawberries,
　hulled and quartered
1 tablespoon sugar
6 ounces fresh raspberries
6 ounces fresh blackberries
6 ounces fresh blueberries
2 mangoes, cubed

MIXED BERRIES AND MANGOES: Toss the strawberries with the sugar in a large bowl. Let stand for 20 minutes. Add the raspberries, blackberries, blueberries and mangoes; toss to coat well.

Fresh lime and lemon
　peel twists
Fresh mint sprigs

TO ASSEMBLE AND SERVE: Invert the mousse onto a serving plate and remove the plastic wrap. Smooth the top and sides with a metal icing spatula. Mound the fruit in the center and around the edge of the mousse. Garnish with lime and lemon twists and mint sprigs.

Mangoes with Ice Cream and Macaroons

*Kathryn Dehlinger, my niece and assistant, and I have laughed out
loud over the original of this recipe. The original two-line recipe passed
on to me by my husband's mother read: Put mashed canned mangoes on
top of ice cream and add crushed macaroons! It has always been a
hit, so I had to include it, but I have embellished it a bit, as you will see.*

1 quart mango ice cream
1 (28-ounce) can mangoes
8 to 10 macaroons, or to taste

Soften the ice cream and scoop into balls with an ice cream scoop. Place in dishes. Drain and coarsely chop the mangoes; crumble the macaroons. Top the ice cream with mangoes and sprinkle with macaroon crumbs. Freeze until serving time. Let stand at room temperature for 5 minutes to serve.

Note: This is beautiful served in a large glass bowl. Pass it at the table and let guests serve themselves.

Ginger Ice Cream

MAKES 1 QUART

*Here is yet another version of vanilla ice cream. This one
basically begins with a crème anglaise.*

1¹/2 cups milk
¹/2 cup heavy cream
³/4 tablespoon minced ginger
¹/4 cup sugar
1 teaspoon vanilla extract
6 egg yolks
¹/2 cup sugar

Combine the milk and cream in a saucepan. Add the ginger, ¹/4 cup sugar and vanilla and mix well. Heat just until scalded. Strain if necessary.

Beat the egg yolks with ¹/2 cup sugar in a mixing bowl for 2 minutes or until well mixed. Add the hot mixture very gradually, stirring constantly; return to the saucepan. Cook over low heat until the mixture coats the back of the spoon, stirring constantly; do not allow to boil. Chill in the refrigerator. Pour into the container of an ice cream freezer and freeze using the manufacturer's directions.

CHOCOLATE PECAN TOFFEE

*We spent Thanksgiving of 2005 in Brady, Texas, at our ranch,
which has been in my husband's family for years. The family gathering
included some in-laws from Abilene; one brought this fabulous
toffee. I had never had it before, but found out at Christmas that it is
now a popular gift item. It can be easily frozen.*

1 cup finely chopped
   pecans, toasted
1 cup (2 sticks) butter
1 cup sugar
1 tablespoon light corn syrup
1/4 cup water
1 to 1 1/2 teaspoons vanilla
   extract
1 cup semisweet chocolate chips
8 to 12 ounces sliced
   almonds, toasted

Spread the pecans in a single layer on a baking sheet
sprayed with nonstick cooking spray. Combine the
butter, sugar, corn syrup and water in a heavy saucepan.
Bring to a boil over medium heat. Cook for 20 to
30 minutes or until golden brown, stirring constantly
and maintaining the mixture at a boil. Stir in the vanilla.

Pour the hot mixture over the pecans and sprinkle
with the chocolate chips. Let stand for 30 minutes,
then smooth the melted chocolate chips over the top.
Sprinkle with the almonds and chill in the refrigerator
for 1 hour or until firm. Break into bite-size pieces and
store in an airtight container.

*NOTE: In April I ate a piece of this wonderful candy left over
from Christmas. Still wonderful!*

CHEESECAKE DREAMS

MAKES 2 DOZEN

*When I began catering twenty years ago, this recipe became a staple
for large buffets. I served it along with a medley of other pick-up
desserts. We all need some of these types of desserts in our repertory.*

---

2 cups all-purpose flour
2/3 cup packed brown sugar
2/3 cup butter, melted
1 cup chopped nuts

DREAM CRUST: Combine the flour, brown sugar, butter and nuts in a food processor and pulse to mix. Press into a baking pan sprayed with nonstick cooking spray. Bake at 350 degrees for 12 to 15 minutes or until light brown. Cool to room temperature.

---

16 ounces cream cheese,
  softened
1/2 cup sugar
2 eggs
1/4 cup milk
1 tablespoon lemon juice
1 teaspoon vanilla extract

CHEESECAKE DREAMS: Combine the cream cheese, sugar, eggs, milk, lemon juice and vanilla in a food processor and process until smooth and creamy. Pour over the dream crust. Bake at 350 degrees for 30 minutes or until set. Cool to room temperature. Store in the refrigerator until chilled or freeze until needed.

TO SERVE: Cut into 2-inch squares and serve cold.

OLD-FASHIONED ROLLED SUGAR COOKIES

MAKES 10 DOZEN SMALL COOKIES

Cooking with the important children in your life is a real gift. I have used this recipe each year to keep first my own children, then my nieces and nephews, and now my grandchildren busy. For the little ones, I prebake the cookies in all sizes and shapes with my collection of cookie cutters. The smaller children love to ice the cookies and sprinkle them with different toppings. It is a joyous occasion for me.

3 cups flour
2 teaspoons baking powder
1/2 teaspoon salt
1 cup (2 sticks) butter
1 1/2 cups sugar
2 eggs
3 teaspoons vanilla extract

SUGAR COOKIES: Sift the flour with the baking powder and salt. Cream the butter and sugar in a mixing bowl until light and fluffy. Beat in the eggs and vanilla. Add the sifted ingredients and mix well. Chill the dough in the refrigerator for 1 to 12 hours. Roll very thin on a lightly floured surface. Cut as desired and place on a cookie sheet sprayed with nonstick cooking spray. Bake at 350 degrees for 6 to 8 minutes or until light brown. Cool on the cookie sheet for several minutes and remove to a wire rack to cool completely.

1/2 cup (1 stick) butter, melted
2 (1-pound) packages
    confectioners' sugar
2 to 3 tablespoons
    vanilla extract
Milk or light cream
Food coloring

CONFECTIONERS' SUGAR ICING: Combine the butter with the confectioners' sugar in a mixing bowl and mix well. Add the vanilla and enough milk to make a smooth paste. Divide the mixture among four bowls and tint each bowl with food coloring. Spoon the icing into separate pastry bags.

TO DECORATE: Spread the cookies with the chosen color of icing and let stand until firm. Pipe the iced cookies with different colored icing to decorate.

NOTE: If the icing is too dry to spread easily, you can thin it with a small amount of hot water.

FRENCH LACE COOKIES

MAKES 12 TO 20

*This is a classic and standard French recipe that can be
changed many ways to vary the cookies. The value of it is that the
cookies can be wrapped around the bottom of a custard cup to make a
basket or rolled into a tube to serve alone or filled with ice cream,
custard, fruit, or any filling of your choice.*

½ cup light corn syrup
¼ cup (½ stick) butter
¼ cup shortening
⅔ cup packed brown sugar
1 cup sifted all-purpose flour
1 cup chopped pecans

Combine the corn syrup, butter, shortening and brown
sugar in a saucepan and bring to a boil, stirring to blend
well. Add the flour and pecans gradually, mixing well.
Drop by rounded teaspoonfuls 3 to 4 inches apart on
a greased cookie sheet. Bake at 325 degrees for 8 to
10 minutes. Cool on the cookie sheet for 30 seconds
to 1 minute and form as desired while still warm; the
cookies will firm up very quickly, so it is best to bake
no more at a time than you can form easily before they
become firm.

*NOTE: You can use this recipe to form cannoli shells for
the Gingersnap Cannoli with Blueberry Lime Filling and
Mango Sauce on page 191.*

221

Things To Know

FOODS

BEEF EXTRACT—Bovril, beef base.

BOVRIL OR DEMI-GLACE—Bovril is a natural beef extract that I frequently use to enrich gravies. Demi-glace Gold and Glace de Poulet Gold are beef and chicken concentrates used in sauces. Forgotten Tradition is another excellent brand of demi-glace. These may be found at gourmet grocery stores or specialty cooking stores such as Williams-Sonoma. Another perfectly acceptable brand, Better than Bouillon, is usually available at local supermarkets.

BREAD CRUMBS—Some recipes call for untoasted, fresh bread crumbs. These are easy to make by putting the bread of choice in a food processor and processing until crumbs form. Crumbs can be frozen, so make more than you need. Canned bread crumbs cannot be substituted for fresh ones.

BUTTER—In all recipes, use unsalted butter. Margarine is not an acceptable substitute.

CANNED VEGETABLES—I do use a few canned vegetables such as black-eyed peas, black beans, great Northern beans, hominy, and tomatoes. Even in Italy, canned tomatoes are acceptable and often preferable.

CHOCOLATE—You only need to use the finest chocolate when it stands alone. If combining chocolate with cream and lots of other ingredients, you can get away with a cheaper chocolate like Baker's, Hershey's, or Nestlé's. When I use white chocolate, I use Lindt or Tobler. Always melt chocolate in a double boiler, as it burns quite easily.

COCONUT MILK—not the liquid inside a coconut, but shredded fresh coconut blended with water, then strained. Do not confuse coconut milk with canned sweetened coconut cream.

CORNSTARCH—Use to thicken gravy. Mix with equal parts water before adding to liquid, then bring to a boil to thicken. May be boiled only once, as sauce will curdle or separate if it is boiled again. To reheat a cornstarch-based sauce, use moderate heat.

CREAM—Heavy cream is also whipping cream. Light cream is also half-and-half.

EGGS—Choose large eggs for using in recipes.

FLOUR—Unless a specific flour is called for, use unbleached white. All-purpose white may be used, but most serious cooks prefer unbleached white.

GARLIC—The size of garlic cloves varies greatly. I suggest using the largest cloves possible. Do not substitute elephant garlic, as it is a different herb altogether.

HERBS—Use fresh herbs whenever possible, unless a recipe specifically calls for dried. (Many herbs, such as basil, taste entirely different when dried. Fresh and dried rosemary, however, are quite similar.) You must use twice the amount of fresh herbs to achieve the same intensity of flavor as a dried herb. Most herbs are easy to grow in pots or a small garden, and make beautiful decorations for platters as well as flavorful additions to food.

KAFFIR LIMES AND LEAVES—Limes are small, with bumpy, wrinkled skin and very little juice. Only rinds and leaves are useful. Leaves have a complex, perfumey citrus aroma. Available at Broadway Central Market. Leaves freeze well. Used mostly for Asian dishes.

KOSHER SALT—This large-grained salt has a flavor that holds up better in stews and other foods that are long cooked.

LEEKS—Leeks are in the onion family. They collect dirt inside and must be washed. To do so, split lengthwise, then wash thoroughly, letting water flow between the layers.

Foods

Lemongrass—This stalk looks like a woody reed. To use, remove tough outer layer and trim root. Smashing the stalk brings out the flavor.

Pepper—Every chef I know recommends only freshly cracked black pepper. I must admit that today I most often use ground pepper but I do not freshly grind it. To me this is certainly permissible for the home cook.

Poblano chile—Used frequently in Mexican and Southwestern cuisine. Darker poblanos are more mature than lighter peppers and are less hot. To tame the heat, soak roasted poblano peppers in salt water.

Stock v. broth—Stock is a term I use to describe a homemade broth. It happens naturally when you cook a chicken in seasoned water. For beef stock, it is necessary to brown beef bones with celery, onion, carrot, bay leaf, thyme, oregano, marjoram, salt, and pepper. Roast in a 350-degree oven for about an hour or until very brown. Deglaze pan with water or any type of alcohol. Cover with water and simmer 3 to 4 hours, adding water as necessary. In the interest of time and convenience however, I have recommended a good canned broth whenever possible. To differentiate, I refer to the homemade version as stock and the canned variety as broth. Be sure when using broth that it is high quality, such as Swanson's. However, brands vary greatly, so try several and pick the one you like the best.

Venison—May be purchased from D'Artagnan. Telephone: 800-DArtagnan.

Wasabi—Japanese horseradish.

Techniques and Terms

Bain marie—a water bath that provides gentle, even heat to delicate foods. To use this technique, place the baking dish in a larger pan and add enough water to rise halfway up the baking dish.

Basic pastry dough—Pastry dough may be made with butter or shortening or a combination. Shortening makes pastry flaky; butter adds taste. There are several variations of pastry dough in this book and they are particularly suited to the specific recipe. The one I have committed to memory and that is my all-purpose personal favorite is this: 1 1/4 cups flour, dash of salt, 8 tablespoons butter, cut into tablespoons, and 1/3 cup cold water. Put flour, butter, and salt in food processor and process until mixture resembles little peas. With machine on, add water. Process only until dough begins to form a ball. Remove dough from processor and form into a ball. Dough is ready to use immediately.

Breading—To get a wonderful crust on fried or sautéed meat or vegetables, dip them first in flour seasoned with salt and pepper, then in lightly beaten egg, and finally in fresh bread crumbs, cracker meal, or coating of choice.

Deglazing—Sautéing meat or poultry leaves flavorful brown bits clinging to the bottom of the pan. Remove the sautéed meat, add some type of liquid, such as wine, brandy, Marsala, etc., and over medium heat, scrape up the brown bits with a spoon or spatula. Add remaining ingredients as specified for the sauce or gravy.

Egg glaze—An egg wash is made by mixing one raw egg with one tablespoon of water. It is brushed over pastry or bread before baking to help it brown. It is also used to glue decorative shapes of dough to bread or pastry.

Emulsify—thickening usually by slowly adding oil or butter to eggs.

Techniques and Terms

FLAMBÉING—Flaming food can be very dangerous. I suggest pouring brandy into a saucepan with no flame under the pan, then igniting the brandy. Flambéing looks showy but is too dangerous for me, so it's not my favorite trick.

FUSION—combining Asian ingredients with ingredients and techniques of other cuisines.

GRAVY—adding broth to a roux

OVEN TEMPERATURE—All restaurants keep ovens at 400 degrees. When in doubt, set the temperature between 350 degrees and 400 degrees. Reheat at 400 degrees.

REDUCING CREAM—When a recipe calls for reducing cream, it's best to do it in a wide-bottomed pan. Use high heat and do not worry; it will not burn. Cream that has been reduced by half will turn a vanilla color. If cream does begin to boil over, whisk it with a balloon whisk to remove some of the air and bring cream back down.

REFRESHING—This technique involves plunging hot food into ice cold water in order to stop the cooking process. It also seals color into green vegetables so they may be prepared well before serving and still retain their color. Today many chefs prefer not to use this technique because they believe it washes out nutrients and flavor. However, when cooking for a large crowd, it is nice to have this technique available.

ROASTING PEPPERS—Wash peppers. Preheat broiler. Place peppers on pan under broiler and roast until charred on all sides. The first side may take 10 to 15 minutes. Turn peppers. The second side will take considerably less time. Place in paper bag or bowl covered with plastic wrap until cool enough to handle. Peel and seed peppers. Use immediately or freeze in plastic freezer bags until needed.

ROUX—A roux is made of equal parts fat and flour and used to thicken a sauce or soup. The basic formula I use is 4 tablespoons butter (or other fat) and 4 tablespoons flour will thicken 3 to 4 cups of liquid. Melt butter in sauté pan, add flour, and cook, stirring, for 1 to 2 minutes or until no traces of flour remain. Add 2 cups liquid all at once. Turn heat to high and whisk until mixture is thick. If mixture becomes too thick, which is probable—and a nice turn of events— thin it down with additional liquid until desired consistency is reached.

SEASONING WITH SALT AND PEPPER—I rarely give specific amounts of salt and pepper. Taste, taste, and taste again. Let this be your guide. Good cooks are not afraid to season generously. Usually, if a dish falls a little flat, it needs more salt.

TO SEASON A WOK:

Fill the wok two-thirds full of water. Place it on its ring on the stove. Add 3/4 cup baking soda and boil for 10 minutes. Discard water. Scrub the wok inside and out with steel wool and hot water. Rinse, then dry with a paper towel.

Set the wok over very low heat. Soak a paper towel with peanut oil and rub the wok, starting with the bottom center and working your way up and out, for about 5 minutes, changing the paper towel as it turns black.

If possible, deep-fry in the wok for its inaugural usage, which will augment the coating.

GENERAL CLEANING INSTRUCTIONS AFTER THE WOK HAS BEEN SEASONED

Using a brush and hot water, scrub the wok. If there are hard blackened bits of food that will not come off, use Chore Boy for copper. Dry. To store a wok best, hang it up if possible.

EQUIPMENT

BLENDER—an essential piece of equipment. It is excellent for puréeing soups and making salsas for many southwestern dishes.

FEEMSTER—a small inexpensive hand-held slicer that makes quick work of slicing vegetables. Newer vegetable slicers are on the market but this is a great stand-by.

FOOD PROCESSOR—This wonderful machine has changed the life of the home cook. I consider it a "must have." Unless I am grating or slicing, I always use the steel blade.

GRILL PAN—a heavy cast-iron skillet with a ridged bottom. I use mine frequently for making attractive grill marks on meat, fish, or vegetables.

HAND-HELD MIXER—a necessity for whipping cream, egg whites, or potatoes.

IMMERSION BLENDER—an electric hand-held mixer.

LARGE STAND MIXER—For heavy-duty mixing and large batches, a stand mixer is much better than an old-fashioned hand-held mixer.

MEAT THERMOMETER—Use an instant read thermometer. Pushed into a piece of meat, it gives an immediate reading. There are many great ones on the market, including special models for meat, poultry, and fish.

MINIATURE FOOD PROCESSOR—This is a great asset and, in my opinion, another "must have." It is handy for making citrus zest, mincing garlic or parsley, and the perfect size for one recipe of vinaigrette. You'll use it every day!

MISCELLANEOUS TOOLS—Every serious cook should have a set of good knives (chef's knife in two sizes, boning knife, and several paring knives), kitchen shears, a mallet for flattening meat, wooden spoons, wire whisks, a strainer and colander, spatulas, pastry brushes, and tweezers for removing small bones from fish.

MOLDS—Many recipes call for 6-ounce ramekins, soufflé dishes, or timbale molds. These are basically one and the same. An excellent source for these molds, along with other cooking equipment, is Bridge Kitchenware in New York City. Call toll free 1-800-BRIDGEK (274-3435). A large assortment of molds, soufflé dishes, pastry forms, etc., opens up endless possibilities for creativity in the kitchen and adds to the joy of cooking. I collect small pastry forms and have found it to be an addictive hobby.

PASTRY BAG—This is one of my favorite toys. Buy the largest pastry bag you can find, plus changeable tips. The basic tips include plain round, fluted, and star shaped. It's nice to have several sizes.

PASTRY CLOTH/ROLLING PIN—A heavy-duty pastry cloth makes rolling pastry a breeze and the work area easy to clean up. I recommend a heavy-duty rolling pin without handles.

PLASTIC SQUEEZE BOTTLES—Filled with sauces, vinaigrettes, or flavored oils, these are great tools for decorating dishes. Buy lots!

SILPAT—A nonstick baking mat made from food-grade silicon. To use, place over a baking sheet. Absolutely nothing will stick to it.

WOK—There are some wonderful woks on the market with flat bottoms that sit nicely on the heating element. They also come with wooden handles that stay cool. These may be purchased at Bridge Kitchenware in New York City, with overnight delivery (1-800-BRIDGEK; 274-3435).

Index

Additional copies of *To Many Cooks* are available
for $25.95 plus postage. Gift sets of Nancy Moorman's
To Many Cooks and her first book, *Memorable Meals,*
are available for $50.00 plus postage.
E-mail: ncwmoorman@sbcglobal.net.